COURSE 1

B

Math in Focus

Singapore Math
by Marshall Cavendish

Extra Practice

Author
Bernice Lau Pui Wah

Marshall Cavendish
Education

U.S. Distributor

Houghton
Mifflin
Harcourt

COMMON
CORE

© 2012 Marshall Cavendish International (Singapore) Private Limited
© 2014 Marshall Cavendish Education Pte Ltd

Published by Marshall Cavendish Education
Times Centre, 1 New Industrial Road, Singapore 536196
Customer Service Hotline: (65) 6213 9688
U.S. Office Tel: (1-914) 332 8888 | Fax: (1-914) 332 8882
E-mail: cs@mceducation.com
Website: www.mceducation.com

Distributed by
Houghton Mifflin Harcourt
222 Berkeley Street
Boston, MA 02116
Tel: 617-351-5000
Website: www.hmheducation.com/mathinfocus

Cover: © Stéphane Maréchal/Photolibrary

First published 2012

Math in Focus® Extra Practice Course 1B
ISBN 978-0-547-57899-6

Printed in Singapore

16 17   1401   19
4500747839   B C D E

Contents

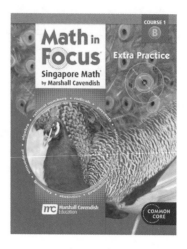

Introducing Math in Focus® Extra Practice

Extra Practice was written to complement *Math in Focus®: Singapore Math® by Marshall Cavendish*. It offers further practice for on-level students and is very similar to the Practice exercises in the Student Books.

Practice to Reinforce and Challenge

Extra Practice provides ample questions to reinforce all concepts taught, and includes challenging questions in the Brain@Work pages. These challenging questions provide extra non-routine problem-solving opportunities, strengthening abstract reasoning powers that include the use of mathematical structures, repeated patterns, models, and tools.

Using the Cumulative Practice

Extra Practice also provides Cumulative Practices that allow students to consolidate learning from several chapters. They can be used to prepare for Benchmark Tests or as another source of good problems for class discussion.

Using the Extra Practice

Extra Practice is an excellent option for homework, or it may be used in class or after school. It is intended for students who simply need more practice to become confident, secure mathematics students who are aiming for excellence.

 Extra Practice is also available online and on the Teacher One Stop.

CHAPTER

Equations and Inequalities

Lesson 8.1   Solving Algebraic Equations

Solve each equation using the substitution method.

1. $x + 8 = 14$

$x =$ _____

2. $y + 6 = 20$

$y =$ _____

3. $p - 9 = 7$

$p =$ _____

4. $k - 15 = 20$

$k =$ _____

5. $6w = 72$

$w =$ _____

6. $15q = 60$

$q =$ _____

7. $\frac{1}{8}e = 7$

$e =$ _____

8. $\frac{1}{10}g = 12$

$g =$ _____

Solve each equation using the concept of balancing.

9. $a + 14 = 20$

$a =$ _____

10. $b + 18 = 34$

$b =$ _____

11. $18 = s - 12$

$s =$ _____

12. $h - 15 = 9$

$h =$ _____

13. $7k = 84$

$k =$ _____

14. $\frac{m}{6} = 16$

$m =$ _____

Name: _____   Date: _____

Solve each equation using the concept of balancing. Write all fractional answers in its simplest form.

15. $x + \dfrac{1}{6} = \dfrac{5}{6}$

16. $y - \dfrac{2}{5} = \dfrac{3}{5}$

$x =$ _____

$y =$ _____

17. $8k = \dfrac{4}{9}$

18. $10g = \dfrac{4}{6}$

$k =$ _____

$g =$ _____

19. $\dfrac{3}{5}p = \dfrac{3}{10}$

20. $\dfrac{2}{3}w = \dfrac{5}{6}$

$p =$ _____

$w =$ _____

21. $x + 1.8 = 3.4$

22. $p + 6.3 = 9.1$

$x =$ _____

$p =$ _____

23. $y - 3.5 = 2.9$

24. $k - 8.5 = 2.7$

$y =$ _____

$k =$ _____

25. $3x + 2.5 = 6.1$

26. $4y - 6.2 = 13$

$x =$ _____

$y =$ _____

27. $3.2k = 40$

28. $2.4p = 36$

$k =$ _____

$p =$ _____

29. $w + \dfrac{2}{3} = 2\dfrac{5}{6}$

30. $d - \dfrac{2}{5} = 1\dfrac{3}{10}$

$w =$ _____

$d =$ _____

31. $\dfrac{3y}{4} = 15$

32. $\dfrac{3}{7}k = 6$

$y =$ _____

$k =$ _____

Solve.

33. Find three whole numbers, such that when inserted into the equation below, the value of $x = 6$.

$$ax + b = c$$

Lesson 8.2   Writing Linear Equations

Solve.

1. Diana has z gerbils. Jackie has 4 times as many gerbils as Diana.
   a) If w stands for the number of gerbils Jackie has, express w in terms of z.

   _____

   b) State the independent and dependent variables in the equation.

   _____

2. Mrs. Boyle buys 2g pounds of beef. Mrs. Anand buys 1.5 pounds less than Mrs. Boyle.
   a) If the amount Mrs. Anand buys is d pounds of beef, express d in terms of g.

   _____

   b) State the independent and dependent variables in the equation.

   _____

3. Adrien has 4 liters of milk. He drinks y liters each day.
   a) If Adrien has x liters of milk left after one week, express x in terms of y.

   _____

   b) State the independent and dependent variables in the equation.

   _____

4. Raul spent b dollars for lunch. Dolly spent $\frac{1}{3}$ of the amount that Raul spent.
   a) If c represents the amount Dolly spent, express c in terms of b.

   _____

   b) State the independent and dependent variables in the equation.

   _____

Name: _____   Date: _____

5. Will earns k dollars a month mowing lawns. He spends 20 dollars and saves the rest. The amount he saves is g dollars.

   a)   Write an equation relating g and k.

_____

   b)   Complete the table to show the relationship between k and g.

Monthly Earnings (k dollars)	100	120	140	150
Savings (g dollars)				

6. The length of a square is p inches. The width of a rectangle is also p inches. The perimeter of a rectangle is 10 inches more than the perimeter of the square. The rectangle has a perimeter of b inches.

   a)   Write an equation relating p and b.

_____

   b)   Complete the table to show the relationship between p and b.

Length of the Square (p inches)	2	4	6	8
Perimeter of the Rectangle (b inches)				

7. It takes Sofia c minutes to cycle from the library to the mall. It takes $\frac{1}{8}$ of the time cycling to travel the same distance walking. Walking takes w minutes.

a) Write an equation relating c and w.

_____

b) Complete the table to show the relationship between c and w.

Cycling (c minutes)	2	3	4	5	6	7
Walking (w minutes)						

c) Graph the relationship between c and w on a coordinate plane.

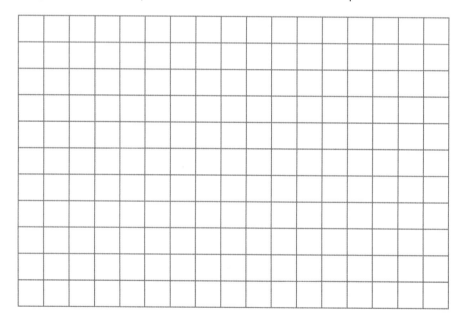

d) Use the graph to find the time it would take Sofia to walk the distance if she cycles it in 44 minutes.

Name: _____   Date: _____

8. Rachel reads *p* books and Malik reads 3 more books than Rachel.
Together they read *h* books.

   a)   Write an equation relating *p* and *h*.

   _____

   b)   Complete the table to show the relationship between *p* and *h*.

Rachel's Books (p)	1	2	3	4	5
Total Number of Books (h)					

   c)   Graph the relationship between *p* and *h* on a coordinate plane.

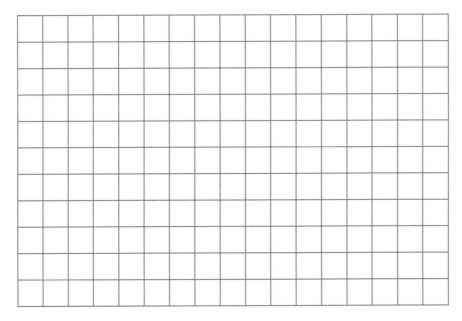

   d)   Use the graph to find how many books Rachael reads if the total number
        of books read is 15.

9. Lynette's mother gives her $80. Lynette spends $5 per day. Lynette has
y dollars left after x days.

   a) Write an equation relating y and x.

   _____

   b) Complete the table to show the relationship between x and y.

Number of Days (x)	1	2	3	4	5	6
Amount of Money Left (y dollars)						

   c) Graph the relationship between x and y on a coordinate plane.

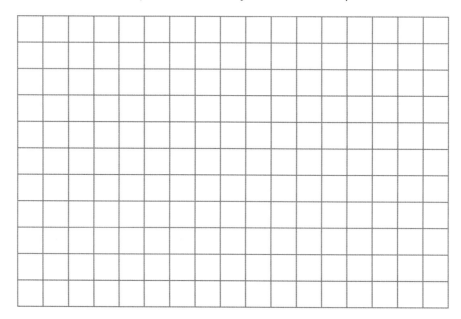

Name: _____   Date: _____

Lesson 8.3   Solving Simple Inequalities

Rewrite each statement using $>$, $<$, $\geq$, or $\leq$.

1. g is less than or equal to 55.

_____

2. q is greater than or equal to 28.

_____

3. p is greater than 15.

_____

4. y is less than 20.

_____

Represent the solutions of each inequality on a number line.

5. $w < 12$

6. $y \geq 6$

7. $z \leq 10$

Write an inequality for each graph on a number line using the variable a.

8.

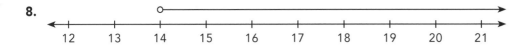

_____

9.

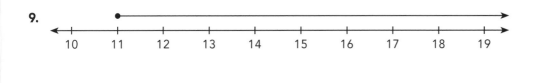

_____

10.

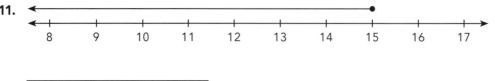

_____

11.

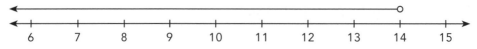

_____

Represent the solutions of each inequality on a number line. Then give three possible integer solutions of each inequality.

12. $w > 4\frac{1}{2}$

13. $k < 10.5$

14. $g \leq 5\frac{3}{4}$

15. $y \geq \frac{9}{10}$

Solve.

16. David's school is more than 8.5 miles from his house. Let x represent the distance between David's house and school.

a) Write an inequality for x. _____

b) Is 8 a possible value of x? Explain. _____

c) Draw a number line to represent the solution set of the inequality. Then state the least possible distance of the school from David's house, as an integer.

17. A small bus can hold a maximum of 20 students. Let y represent the number of students.

a) Write an inequality for y. _____

b) Is 18 a possible value of y? Explain. _____

c) Draw a number line to represent the solution set of the inequality. Then state the maximum value of y.

Each inequality has the variable on the right side of the inequality symbol. Graph each solution on a number line.

18. $9 > m$

19. $-15 \geq k$

20. $-3\frac{1}{2} \leq t$

21. $3.5 < c$

Lesson 8.4   Real-World Problems: Equations and Inequalities

**Write and solve an algebraic equation or inequality for each problem.
Show your work.**

1. When a number is doubled, the result is 48. What is the number?

2. After students borrowed 28 novels from the school library, there were 35 novels left.
   How many novels were in the school library at first?

3. In a swimming class, $\frac{2}{5}$ of the participants are girls. There are 24 boys in the class.
   Find the total number of participants in the class.

4. Claire jogs around an oval track and is able to complete one lap in 5 minutes.
   If she jogs at the same pace for 42 minutes, how many laps would she be able
   to jog? Write an inequality and find the number of whole laps Claire completes.

5. A box can hold a maximum of 60 comic books. If comic books are bundled together in groups of 8, write and solve an inequality to find the maximum number of bundles of comic books that the box can carry.

6. When a number is tripled and 8 is subtracted from the result, the answer is 16. What is the number?

7. The difference of two numbers is 117. The greater number is 4 times the other number. What is the smaller number?

8. Jason's age is 3 times Shauna's present age. In 4 years' time, the sum of their ages will be 56 years. Find their present ages.

9. Mrs. Jones buys 7 T-shirts and 6 hats for $86. The price of each T-shirt is $3 more than the price of each hat. How much does Mrs. Jones pay for each item?

10. For every 15 students on a field trip, there needs to be one teacher. How many teachers are needed for a group of 100 students?

11. Karen has some lawn chairs. Jenny has twice as many lawn chairs as Karen, and Rico has 3 more lawn chairs than Karen. Together, they have a total of 31 lawn chairs. How many lawn chairs does Karen have?

12. Jared has some quarters and dimes that total $5.50. If he has 8 more quarters than dimes, how many dimes does Jared have?

CHAPTER

 Brain @ Work

1. Montell is 30 years younger than his mother. In 5 years, Montell's age will be $\frac{1}{3}$ of his mother's age. Find Montell's mother's age now.

2. The length of a rectangle is twice its width. If the perimeter of the rectangle is less than 74 inches, find its maximum whole-number width.

CHAPTER

The Coordinate Plane

Lesson 9.1   Points on the Coordinate Plane

Use the coordinate plane below.

1.   Give the coordinates of each point.

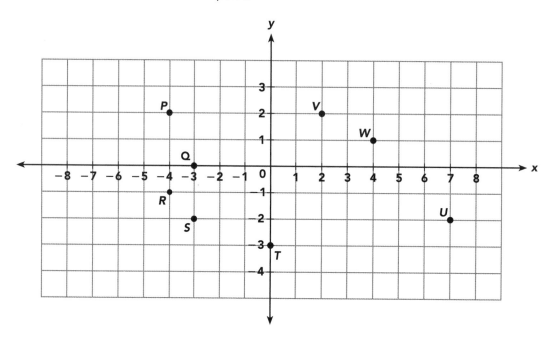

Plot the points on the coordinate plane below. In which quadrant is each point located?

2.   S (3, 2), T (0, −1), U (−4, −2), V (4, 0), W (−2, 1), and Z (2, −2)

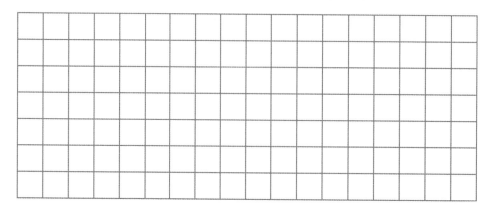

Name: _____   Date: _____

Points *R* and *S* are reflections of each other about the y-axis. Use the coordinate plane below. Give the coordinates of point *S* if the coordinates of point *R* are the following:

3. (3, 9) _____

4. (−7, 4) _____

5. (−5, −6) _____

6. (8, −2) _____

Points *P* and *Q* are reflections of each other about the x-axis. Use the coordinate plane below. Give the coordinates of point *Q* if the coordinates of point *P* are the following:

7. (3, 9) _____

8. (−7, 4) _____

9. (−5, −6) _____

10. (8, −2) _____

About which axis are the following coordinates reflections of each other?

11. (−2, 0) and (2, 0)

12. (−8, −8) and (−8, 8)

_____

_____

For each exercise, plot the given points on a coordinate plane. Then join the points in order with line segments to form a closed figure. Name each figure formed.

13. A (−3, −1), B (3, −1), C (3, 5), and D (−3, 5)

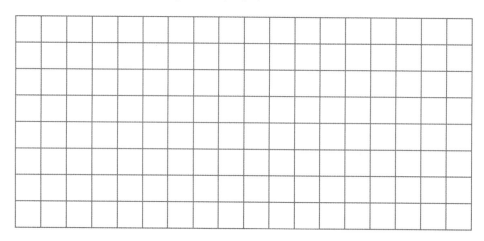

Figure formed: _____

14. A (0, 4), B (2, −2), and C (5, 1)

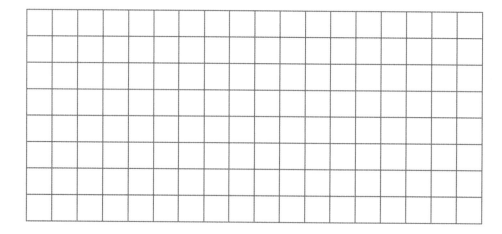

Figure formed: _____

15. *P* (0, 0), *Q* (4, 3), *R* (3, 6), and *S* (−1, 3)

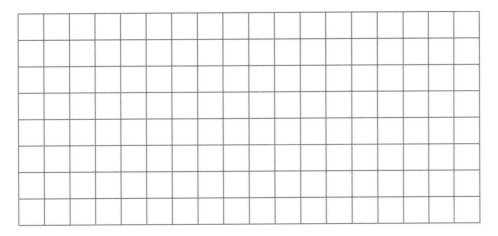

Figure formed: _____

16. *P* (1, −2), *Q* (3, 2), *R* (−4, 2), and *S* (−2, −2)

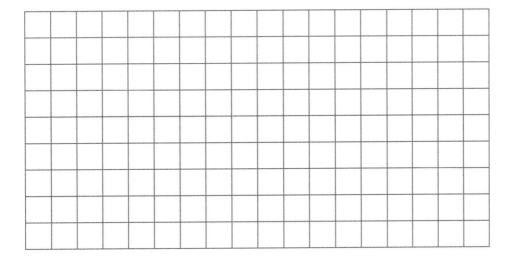

Figure formed: _____

Plot the points on a coordinate plane and answer each question.

17. **a)** Plot points P (−3, 0), R (1, −2), and S (0, 1).
    b) Figure $PQRS$ is a square. Plot point Q and give its coordinates.
    c) Figure $PRST$ is a parallelogram. Plot point T above $\overline{PS}$ and give its coordinates.

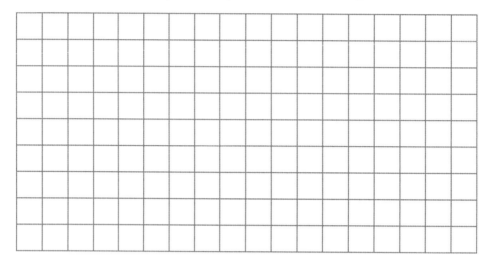

18. **a)** Plot points A (−2, −3), B (4, −3), and C (1, 4)
    b) What kind of triangle is triangle ABC?
    c) Figure $ABCD$ is a parallelogram. Plot point D and give its coordinates.

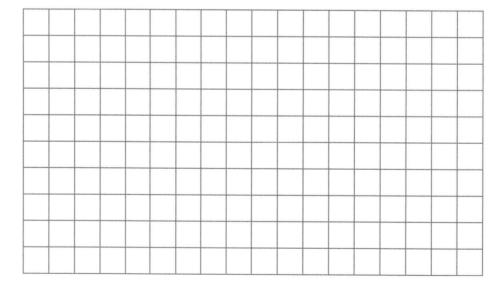

Name: _____   Date: _____

Lesson 9.2 Length of Line Segments

Plot each pair of points on the coordinate plane below. Connect the points to form a line segment and find its length.

1. A (6, 2) and B (6, −3)

2. C (−4, 0) and D (3, 0)

3. E (−5, 3) and F (1, 3)

4. G (−2, 3) and H (−2, −3)

5. J (0, 2) and K (0, −3)

6. M (4, −1) and N (4, −4)

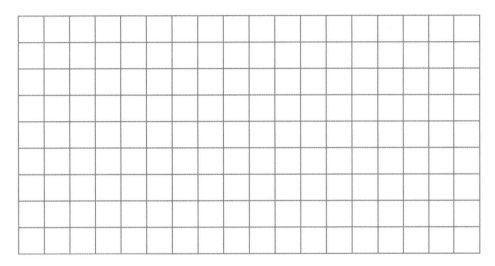

Find the coordinates.

7. Rectangle ABCD is plotted on a coordinate plane. The coordinates of point A are (1, −1), and the coordinates of point D are (1, 2). Each unit on the coordinate plane represents 1 centimeter, and the perimeter of rectangle ABCD is 18 centimeters. Find the coordinates of points B and C given these conditions:
    a)   Points B and C are to the right of points A and D.
    b)   Points B and C are to the left of points A and D.

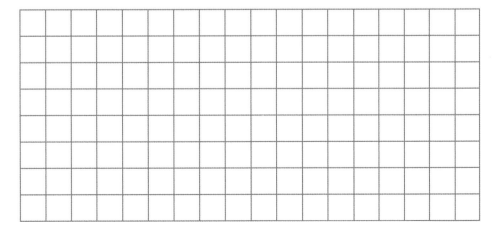

8. Square *EFHG* is plotted on a coordinate plane. The coordinates of point *E* are
    (−2, 1) and the coordinates of point *F* are (2, 1). Find the coordinates of points
    G and *H* given these conditions:
    a) Points *G* and *H* are above points *E* and *F*.
    b) Points *G* and *H* are below points *E* and *F*.

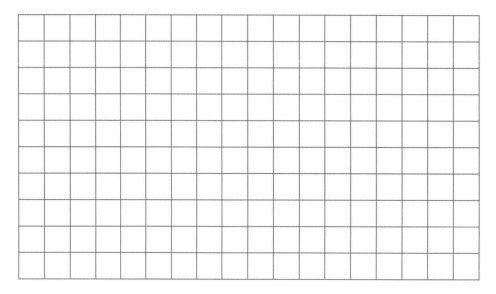

9. Triangle *ABC* is plotted on a coordinate plane. The coordinates of point *A* are
    (−2, 2), the coordinates of point *B* are (6, 2), and the coordinates of point *C*
    are (6, 5).
    a) What type of triangle is triangle *ABC*?
    b) Figure *ABCD* is a rectangle. Plot point *D* on the coordinate plane
    and give its coordinates.

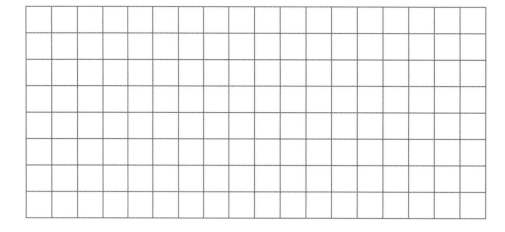

Name: _____ Date: _____

In the diagram, figure *PQRSTU* represents a field. The side length of each grid square is 5 feet. Use the diagram to answer questions 10 to 13.

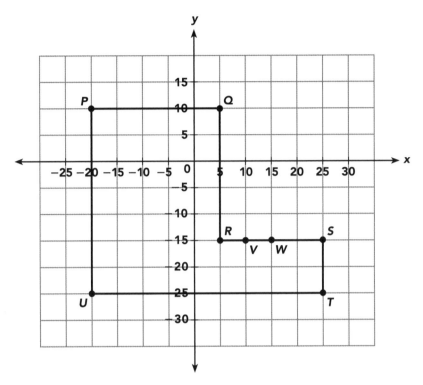

10. Give the coordinates of points *P*, *Q*, *R*, *S*, *T*, and *U*.

11. James and Rita build a picket fence around the field. They leave a 5-foot opening for the gate. What is the total length of the fence?

12. The gate, $\overline{VW}$, lies on $\overline{RS}$ and is 10 feet from point *S*. Give the coordinates of points *V* and *W*.

13. Find the area of the field.

Name: _____   Date: _____

In the diagram, figure *ABC* represents a playground. The side length of each grid square is 4 yards. Use the diagram to answer questions 14 to 17.

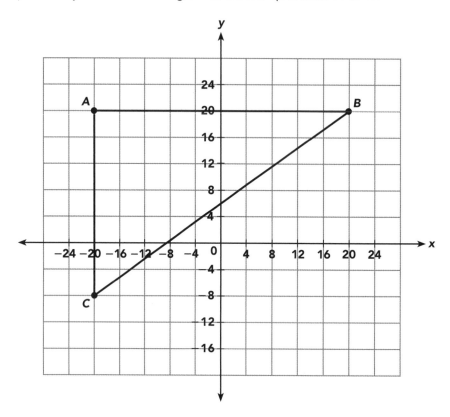

14. Give the coordinates of points *A*, *B*, and *C*.

15. There is a square sandbox *DEFG* in the playground. Point *D* is 20 yards from point *A*. $\overline{DE}$ is 8 yards in length. $\overline{EF}$ is also 8 yards in length and is parallel to $\overline{AC}$. Plot and label points *D*, *E*, *F*, and *G* on the coordinate plane.

16. If *BC* is approximately 49 yards, what is the perimeter of the playground?

17. Tonya starts at point *E* and rides her scooter to point *A* then to point *C*. She continues around the perimeter of the playground toward point *B*. If she travels at 5 yards per second, how many seconds will it take her to get to point *B*?

Name: _____   Date: _____

Lesson 9.3   Real-World Problems: Graphing

Solve.

1. The number of figurines, *d*, that Jenna can paint in *h* hours is given by
    d = 12*h*. Graph the relationship between *h* and *d*. Use 2 units on the horizontal
    axis to represent 1 hour and 1 unit on the vertical axis to represent 6 figurines.

Time (*h* hours)	1	2	3	4	5
Number of Figurines (*d*)	12		36		

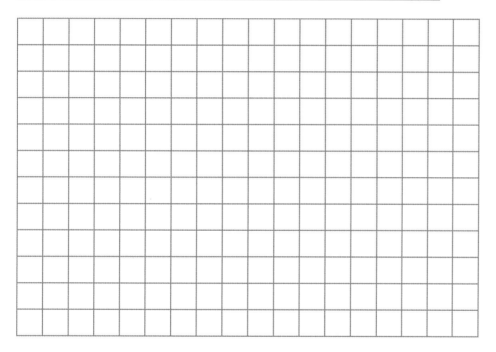

a)   What type of graph is it?

b)   How many figurines can Jenna paint in 2.5 hours?

c)   How long will it take Jenna to paint 54 figurines?

d)   If Jenna has to paint at least 48 figurines, how many hours will she need to
     paint? Express your answer in the form of an inequality where *h* stands for
     the amount of time.

e)   Name the dependent and independent variables.

2. Water is being drained from a fish tank. The water level y centimeters, at time x minutes, is given by $y = 60 - 5x$. Complete the table. Graph the relationship between x and y. Use 1 unit on the horizontal axis to represent 1 minute and 2 units on the vertical axis to represent 10 centimeters.

a)

Time (x minutes)	2	4	6	8	10
Water Level (y centimeters)	50			20	

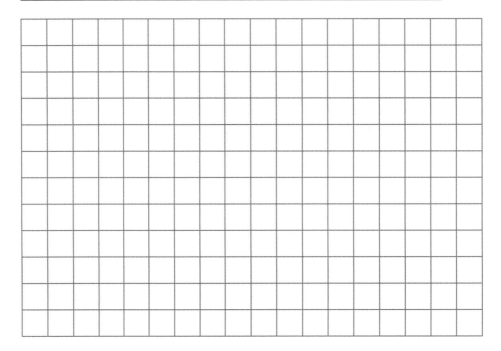

b)   What is the water level at 3 minutes?

c)   In how many minutes will the water level be 25 centimeters?

d)   How long will it take to drain all the water from the tank?

e)   What is the average drainage rate of the fish tank?

Name: _____   Date: _____

3. The fee C dollars a certain electrician charges is given by $C = 30t + 20$, where t is the number of hours the electrician spends on the job. Complete the table. Graph the relationship between C and t. Use 2 units on the horizontal axis to represent 1 hour and 1 unit on the vertical axis to represent $20.

a)

Time (t hours)	0	1	2	3	4
Cost (C dollars)	20	50			

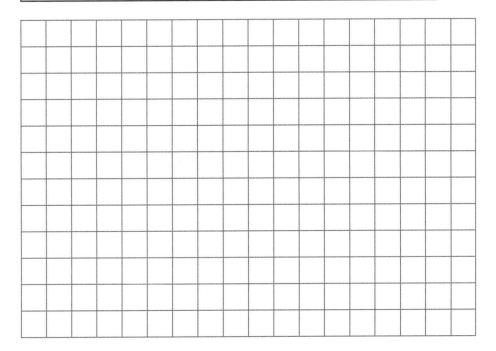

b) Find the fee the electrician charges for a 1.5-hour job.

c) The electrician charges $95 for a job. Based on the graph, how many hours did it take the electrician to complete the job?

d) What is the electrician's average hourly rate if the electrician is paid $95 for a job?

e) What is the minimum fee the electrician charges for any job? Express your answer in the form of an inequality in terms of C, where C stands for the amount of money.

CHAPTER

Brain @ Work

1. **a)** Plot each set of points on a coordinate plane. Then join the points in order with line segments to form a closed figure and label it. Name each figure formed.

   i. $A\,(-1, 0)$, $B\,(0, -1)$, $C\,(1, 0)$, $D\,(0, 1)$
   ii. $E\,(-2, 0)$, $F\,(0, -2)$, $G\,(2, 0)$, $H\,(0, 2)$
   iii. $J\,(-3, 0)$, $K\,(0, -3)$, $M\,(3, 0)$, $N\,(0, 3)$

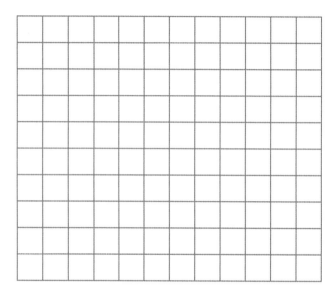

Figure formed:

i.   _____

ii.   _____

iii. _____

   b) Find the area of figures *ABCD*, *EFGH*, and *JKMN* if each unit on the coordinate plane represents 1 centimeter.

   c) What conclusion can you draw about the relationship among the areas of figures *ABCD*, *EFGH*, and *JKMN*?

CHAPTER

Area of Polygons

Lesson 10.1   Area of Triangles

Identify a base and a height for each triangle.

1.
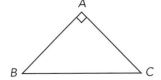

2.
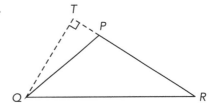

For each triangle, label a base with the letter *b* and a height with the letter *h*.

3.
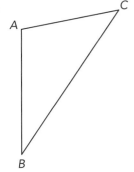

4.
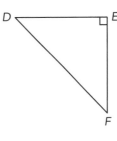

5.
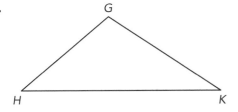

6.
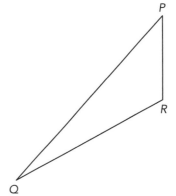

Name: _____   Date: _____

Find the area of each triangle.

7.

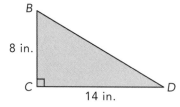

B, 8 in., C, 14 in., D

8.

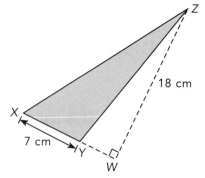

Z, 18 cm, X, 7 cm, Y, W

The area of each triangle is 96 square centimeters. Find the height.

9.

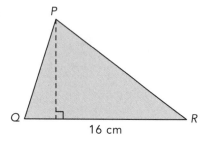

P, Q, 16 cm, R

10.

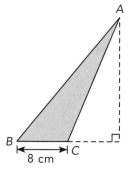

A, B, 8 cm, C

The area of each triangle is 135 square yards. Find the base.

11.

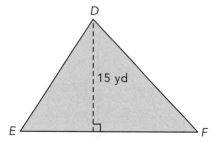

D, 15 yd, E, F

12.

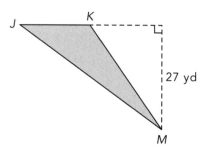

J, K, 27 yd, M

Name: _____   Date: _____

Solve. Show your work.

13. Triangle *PQR* is a section of a ball field. Find the area of triangle *PQR*.

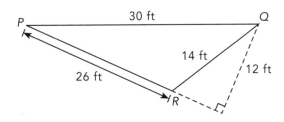

14. The area of triangle *AEC* is 28 square inches. Find the area of the unshaded region of rectangle *ABCD*.

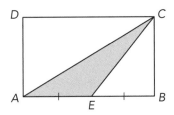

15. Rectangle *EFGH* is divided into six identical rectangles. Find the area of the shaded region.

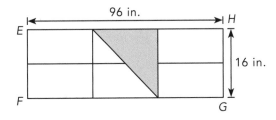

16. Triangle *XYZ* is a right triangle. Triangle *WXY* is an isosceles triangle.
Find the area of triangle *WXY*.

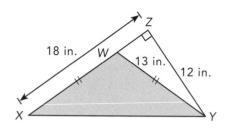

17. Figure *EFGH* is a rectangle. Point *M* is the mid-point of $\overline{FG}$.
If *EF* = *FM*, what is the area of triangle *EMN*?

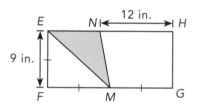

Solve.

18. The coordinates of the vertices of a triangle are *A* (6, 1), *B* (1, 1),
and *C* (1, 5). Find the area of triangle *ABC*.

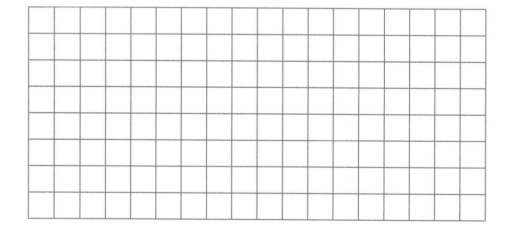

19. The coordinates of the vertices of a triangle are $P\,(-4, -5)$, $Q\,(-6, -1)$, and $R\,(2, -1)$. Find the area of triangle PQR.

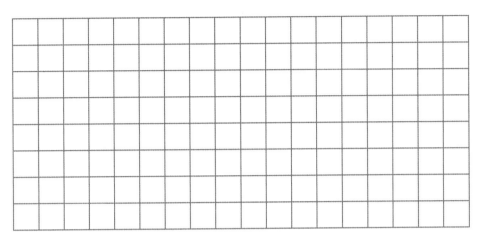

20. The coordinates of the vertices of a triangle are $X\,(8, 4)$, $Y\,(1, 0)$, and $Z\,(1, 6)$. Find the area of triangle XYZ.

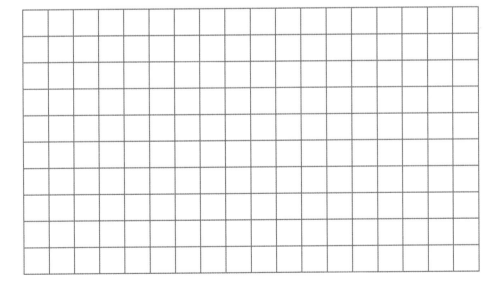

21. The coordinates of the vertices of a triangle are D (−5, 3), E (−5, −2), and F (4, −1). Find the area of triangle DEF.

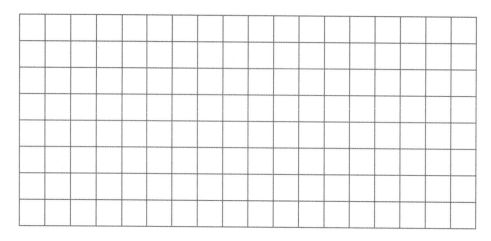

22. The coordinates of the vertices of a triangle are L (−9, 5), M (−3, 0), and N (1, 0). Find the area of triangle LMN. (Hint: Draw a rectangle around triangle LMN.)

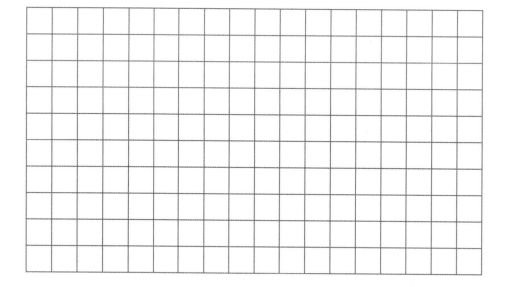

Name: _____   Date: _____

23. The coordinates of the vertices of a triangle are G (−4, −3), H (2, 2), and K (5, 2).
Find the area of triangle *GHK*.

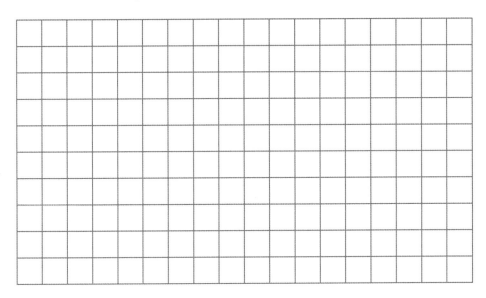

Solve. Show your work.

24. Figure *DEFGHK* is made up of two squares and a triangle. The areas of the
squares are 144 square inches and 64 square inches. Find the area of the figure.

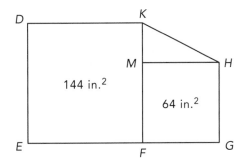

25. Square *PQRS* has a perimeter of 160 inches. Point *M* is the midpoint of $\overline{QR}$, and point *N* is the midpoint of $\overline{SR}$. Find the area of triangle *PMN*.

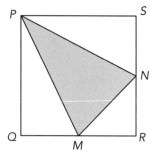

26. A right triangle has a height of 16 inches and a base of 12 inches. Four such triangles are arranged to form a large square with a small square at the center, as shown. Find the side length of the larger square.

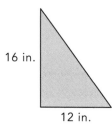

16 in.

12 in.

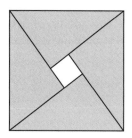

Name: _____   Date: _____

Lesson 10.2   Area of Parallelograms and Trapezoids

For each parallelogram, draw and label the height *h* for the given base *b*.

1.

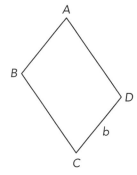

2.

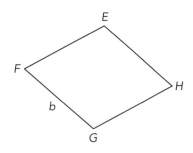

For each parallelogram, label a base and a height. Use *b* and *h*.

3.

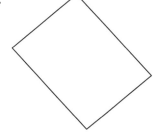

4.

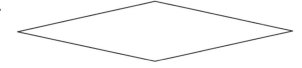

Find the area of each parallelogram.

5.

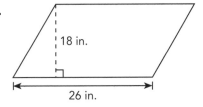

6.

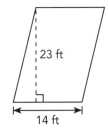

For each trapezoid, label the height and bases. Use h, b_1, and b_2.

7.

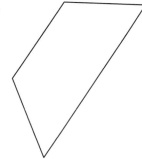

8.

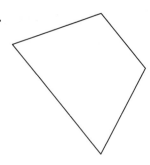

Find the area of each trapezoid.

9.

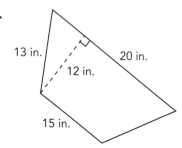

13 in.   20 in.

12 in.

15 in.

10.

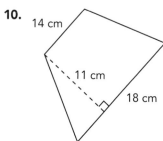

14 cm

11 cm

18 cm

Solve. Show your work.

11. The area of parallelogram *EFGH* is 207 square inches. Its height is 9 inches. Find the length of $\overline{GH}$.

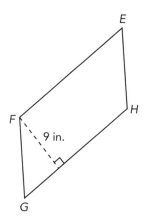

E

F   *H*

9 in.

G

12. The area of parallelogram *ABCD* is 112 square inches. The length of $\overline{BC}$ is 16 inches. Find the height.

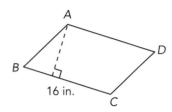

13. The area of trapezoid *PQRS* is 108 square centimeters. Find the height.

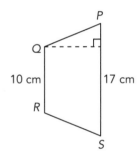

14. The area of trapezoid *WXYZ* is 375 square feet. Find the height.

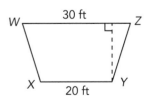

Solve.

15. Three out of the four coordinates of the vertices of a parallelogram are A (0, 3), B (−3, −2), and D (5, 3). Plot the coordinates on the coordinate plane. Find the coordinates of point C. Then find the area of parallelogram $ABCD$.

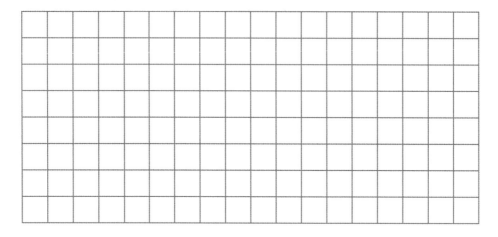

16. The coordinates of the vertices of a trapezoid are P (−4, −1), Q (5, −1), R (3, 4), and S (0, 4). Plot the coordinates on the coordinate plane. Find the area of trapezoid $PQRS$.

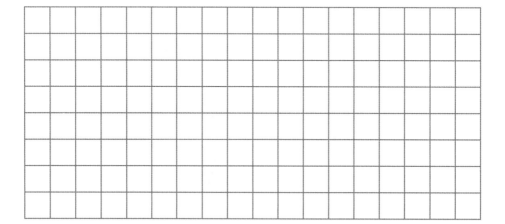

Name: _____   Date: _____

Solve. Show your work.

17. The area of trapezoid *JKMN* is 136 square miles. Its height is 8 miles. Find the length of $\overline{JN}$.

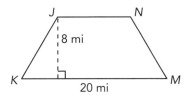

18. Trapezoid *ABCD* is made up of triangles *ABC* and *ADC*. The area of trapezoid *ABCD* is 312 square yards. Find the area of triangle *ABC*.

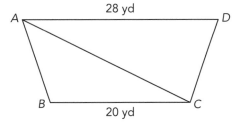

Lesson 10.3   Area of Other Polygons

Give the minimum number of identical triangles you could divide each regular polygon into so that you could find the area of the polygon.

1.

2.
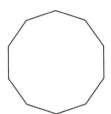

Use the given information to find the area of each regular polygon.

3.
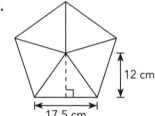

12 cm

17.5 cm

4.
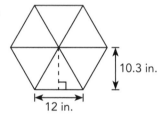

10.3 in.

12 in.

Solve.

5. A playground in the shape of a regular pentagon has an area of 292.5 square feet. Find the length of each side of the playground.

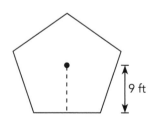

9 ft

6. A wooden frame in the shape of a regular hexagon is 93.6 square inches. The
    length of each side of the hexagon is 6 inches. Find the height of the hexagon.

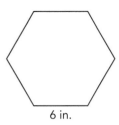

6 in.

7. A regular hexagon is formed by 3 identical rhombuses. The height of each
    rhombus is 6 centimeters and its base is 7 centimeters. Find the area of the
    hexagon.

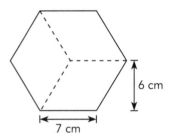

6 cm

7 cm

8. Find the area of the regular polygon.

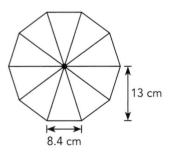

13 cm

8.4 cm

9. Use the given information to find the area of the regular polygon *ABCDEFGH*.

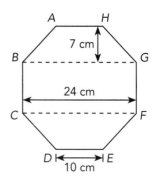

10. The figure is formed by a regular pentagon and a triangle. Find the area of the figure.

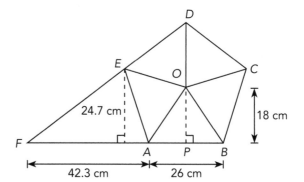

Name: _____   Date: _____

Lesson 10.4   Area of Composite Figures

Draw straight lines to divide each figure. Describe two ways to find the area of each figure.

1. Divide the figure into two triangles.

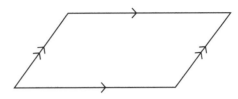

2. Divide the figure into two triangles.

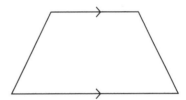

3. Divide the figure into an isosceles triangle, two right triangles, and a rectangle.

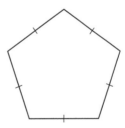

Draw straight lines to divide. Describe a way to find the area of each figure.

4.

5.

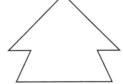

Solve.

6. a) Plot points *A* (−3, 6), *B* (−3, −3), *C* (2, −1), *D* (6, −1), and *E* (2, 4) on a coordinate plane.

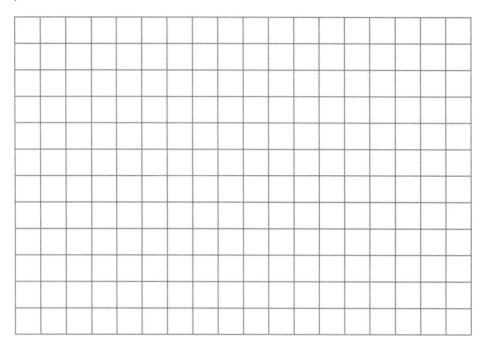

b) Find the area of figure *ABCDE*.

c) Point *F* lies on $\overline{EC}$. The area of triangle *EDF* is $\frac{3}{5}$ the area of triangle *EDC*.

Give the coordinates of point *F*. Plot point *F* on the coordinate plane. Draw a segment joining points *D* and *F* and shade triangle *EDF*.

7. Parallelogram *PQRS* is made up of a trapezoid and a triangle. The area of triangle *PQT* is 28 square centimeters. Find the height of the triangle. Then find the area of parallelogram *PQRS*.

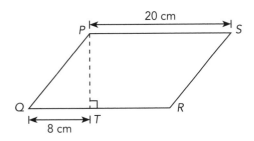

8. The figure is made up of square *CDEF* and trapezoid *ABCF*. Find the area of the figure.

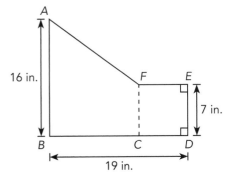

9. The figure is formed by trapezoid *QRST* and parallelogram *PQTU*.
Find the area of the figure.

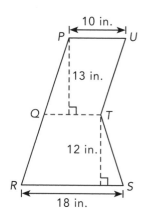

10. Trapezoid *ABDE* is made up of parallelogram *ABCE* and triangle *CDE*.
The area of parallelogram *ABCE* is 135 square inches. Find the area of triangle
CDE. Then find the area of trapezoid *ABDE*.

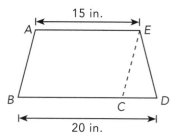

11. The figure below is formed by overlapping four identical square cards
in a certain way. Each square card has a length of 6 centimeters.
Find the area of the figure.

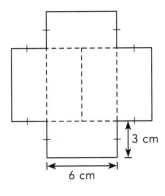

3 cm

6 cm

12. $\frac{3}{8}$ of the square is shaded. Find the area of the shaded region.

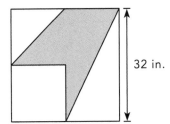

32 in.

13. The figure is formed by two identical squares with a side length of 16 inches. The ratio of the area of the shaded region to the unshaded region of the figure is 1 : 14. Find the area of the unshaded region.

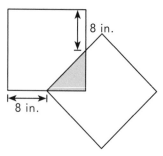

14. The figure is made up of two squares and a right triangle. Find the area of the shaded region.

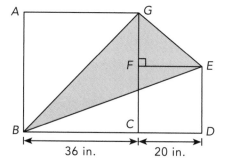

15. Rectangle *PQRS* is formed by putting 9 identical small rectangles together
without overlapping. The perimeter of the figure is 138 inches.

    a)   Find the area of each small rectangle.

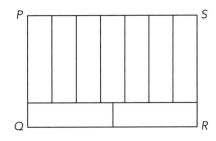

    b)   Find the area of rectangle *PQRS*.

16. Paul draws a rectangle *ABCD* with a perimeter of 30 inches. He then draws
a square on each side of the rectangle, as shown. The total area of the four
squares is 234 square inches. What is the area of rectangle *ABCD*?

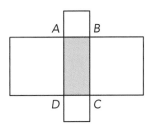

CHAPTER

10 Brain @ Work

1. Triangle *ABC* and triangle *XYZ* are equilateral triangles, each having an area of 18 square centimeters. Each side of each triangle is divided into three equal parts, as shown.

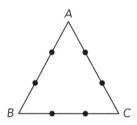   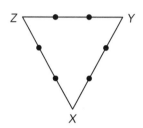

When triangle *ABC* and triangle *XYZ* intersect, a composite figure is formed as shown below.

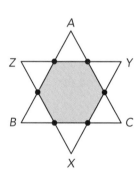

a)   Find the area of the shaded region

b)   Find the area of the composite figure.

2. Rectangle *PQRS* has a length of 18 inches and a width of 12 inches.
Each side is divided into three equal sections.

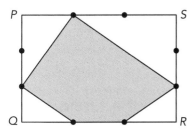

a)   Find the area of the shaded region.

b)   In the rectangle *PQRS*, $\overline{MN}$ is drawn to meet $\overline{QR}$ at point *N* such that the shaded region is divided into two equal parts. Find the length of $\overline{QN}$.

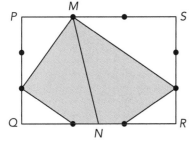

CHAPTER

11 Circumference and Area of a Circle

Lesson 11.1 Radius, Diameter, and Circumference of a Circle

Find the circumference of each circle. Use 3.14 as an approximation for π.

1.
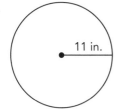

2.
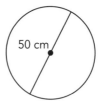

Find the distance around each semicircle. Use $\frac{22}{7}$ as an approximation for π.

3.
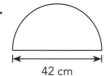

4.
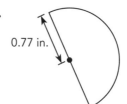

Find the distance around each quadrant. Use 3.14 as an approximation for π.

5.

6.

Name: _____ Date: _____

Solve. Show your work. Use $\frac{22}{7}$ as an approximation for π.

7. A circular tabletop has a radius of 1.9 feet. Find its circumference.

8. A circular window has a diameter of 25 inches. Find its circumference.

9. The diameter of a coin is 18 millimeters. Find its circumference.

10. A sink is in the shape of a semicircle. Find the distance around the sink.

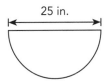

25 in.

11. A coin purse is shaped like a quadrant. Find the distance around the purse.

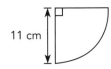

11 cm

Find the distance around each figure. Use 3.14 as an approximation for π.

12. The figure is made up of a semicircle and a quadrant.

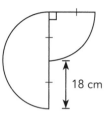

18 cm

13. The figure is made up of four identical quadrants.

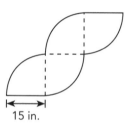

15 in.

14. The figure is made up of a semicircle and two identical equilateral triangles.

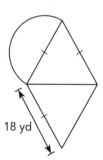

18 yd

15. The figure is made up of a quadrant within a square. Find the distance around the shaded region.

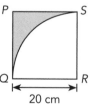

P   S

Q   R

20 cm

Name: _____   Date: _____

Find the distance around each figure. Use $\frac{22}{7}$ as an approximation for π.

16. The figure is made up of two identical semicircles enclosed within a rectangle.

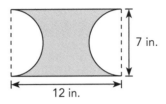

7 in.

12 in.

17. The figure is made up of two semicircles.

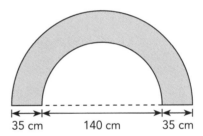

35 cm   140 cm   35 cm

18. The figure is made up of two identical quadrants.

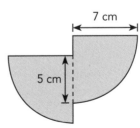

7 cm

5 cm

Lesson 11.2   Area of a Circle

Find the area of each circle. Use 3.14 as an approximation for π.

1.

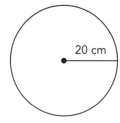

20 cm

2.

8 mi

Find the area of each semicircle. Use $\frac{22}{7}$ as an approximation for π.

3.

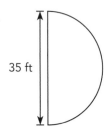

35 ft

4.

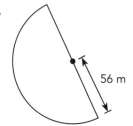

56 m

Find the area of each quadrant to the nearest tenth. Use 3.14 as an approximation for π.

5.

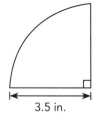

3.5 in.

6.

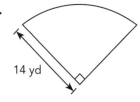

14 yd

Name: _____   Date: _____

Solve. Show your work. Use $\frac{22}{7}$ as an approximation for π.

7. A park is in the shape of a semicircle. Find the area of the park.

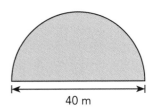

40 m

8. The shape of a soap dish is a semicircle. Find the area of the soap dish.

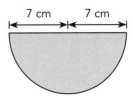

7 cm   7 cm

9. A 6-inch pizza costs $3.50. A 12-inch pizza costs $11.

    a) How much less is the area of the 6-inch pizza than the area of the 12-inch pizza? Express your answer to the nearest hundredth.

    b) Which is the better deal? Explain your reasoning.

Name: _____   Date: _____

10. The figure shows a circular fishpond enclosed within a semicircular flowerbed. The diameter of the pond, $\overline{PQ}$, is 42 inches. Find the area of the shaded region.

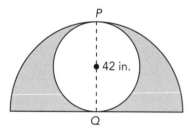

11. The figure is made up of two identical quadrants and a square. Find the area of the shaded region.

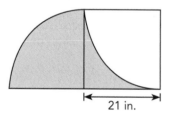

21 in.

Solve. Show your work. Use 3.14 as an approximation for π.

12. The figure is made up of a semicircle and two identical quadrants. Point A is the center of the semicircle. Find the area of the figure.

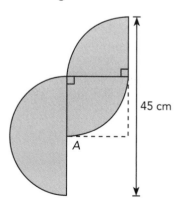

45 cm

A

13. The figure is made up of a semicircle in a quadrant. Find the area of the shaded region.

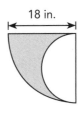

18 in.

14. The figure shows a circle and four identical semicircles inside it. Point *C* is the center of the circle and $\overline{AE}$ is the diameter. If *AE* = 48 centimeters, find the area of the shaded region.

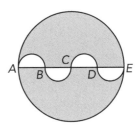

15. The figure shows two circles. Points *A* and *B* are the centers of the circles. The area of the shaded region is $\frac{2}{7}$ the area of the smaller circle. Find the total area of the unshaded region of the figure.

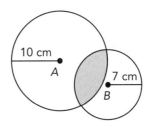

10 cm

7 cm

Lesson 11.3   Real-World Problems: Circles

Solve. Show your work.

1. The diameter of a circular tablecloth is 72 inches. Find its area and circumference. Use 3.14 as an approximation for π.

2. The radius of a circular carpet is 1.2 meters. Find its area and circumference to the nearest hundredth. Use 3.14 as an approximation for π.

3. A piece of wire is wound exactly 100 times, without overlap, around a circular tube with a radius of 9.8 centimeters. Find the length of the piece of wire in meters. Use $\frac{22}{7}$ as an approximation for π.

9.8 cm

4. The diameter of a bicycle wheel is 0.7 meter. Find the number of complete revolutions made by the wheel if the bicycle travels 440 meters. Use $\frac{22}{7}$ as an approximation for π.

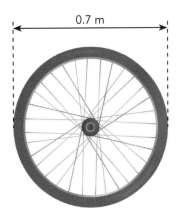

0.7 m

5. A walkway is formed by four semicircles as shown below. The diameter of the inner semicircles is 14 feet. The width between the outer and inner semicircles is 2 feet. Find the area of the walkway. Use 3.14 as an approximation for π.

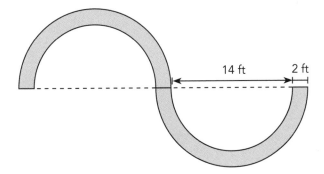

14 ft   2 ft

6. A rug is formed by four identical quadrants as shown below.
   a) Find the distance around the shaded part of the rug.
   Use 3.14 as an approximation for π.

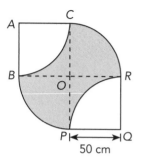

50 cm

   b) Find the area of the shaded part of the rug.

7. The design shown is made up of two circles and two quadrants. The diameter of the larger circle is twice the diameter of the smaller circle. The larger circle has a diameter of 56 centimeters. Find the area of the shaded region. Use 3.14 as an approximation for π.

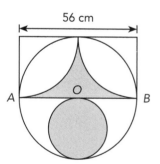

56 cm

8. Alex wants to cut out as many circular badges as possible from a rectangular sheet of cardboard. The diameter of each badge is 14 centimeters. Use $\frac{22}{7}$ as an approximation for π.

a) How many badges can Alex cut?

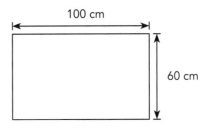

100 cm

60 cm

b) What is the area of the cardboard left over?

9. The diagram shows a running track made up of a rectangle with semicircles at the two ends. Its two lanes are 3.5 meters apart. Adam and Joe run round the track twice in separate lanes.

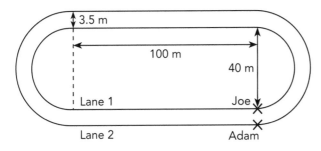

3.5 m

100 m

40 m

Lane 1

Joe

Lane 2

Adam

a) Who runs farther? Use $\frac{22}{7}$ as an approximation for π.

b) How much farther does he run?

CHAPTER

1. The figure shows a square *ABCD* and a quadrant. Point *A* is the center of the quadrant and *BD* is 10 centimeters long. Find the area of the shaded region. Use 3.14 as an approximation for π.

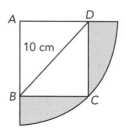

2. The figure shows a circle that touches each square at exactly four points. The length of square *PQRS* is 8 inches. Find the area of square *ABCD*. Use 3.14 as an approximation for π.

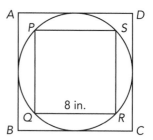

Name: _____   Date: _____

3. The figure shows three overlapping semicircles enclosed within square *PQRS*.
   Find the area of the shaded region. Use $\frac{22}{7}$ as an approximation for π.

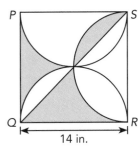

4. The shaded regions of the figure are four flowerbeds enclosing a fishpond at
   the center. The flowerbeds are formed by four identical quadrants with centers
   at points *A*, *B*, *C*, and *D*. Use $\frac{22}{7}$ as an approximation for π.

   a) Find the area of the fishpond.

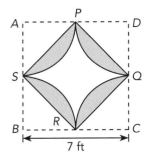

   b) Find the total area of the 4 flowerbeds.

Cumulative Practice
for Chapters 8 to 11

Represent the solution set of each inequality on a number line.

1. $w > -15$

2. $x \geq 8\frac{1}{2}$

3. $y \leq 12.25$

4. $z < -\frac{1}{3}$

Plot the points on the coordinate plane below and answer each question.

5. a) Points R and S are reflections of each other about the y–axis. What are the coordinates of point S if point R is located at $(-4, 1)$? Connect the two points to form a line segment.

b) Point T lies below $\overline{RS}$ and forms a right angle RST. $\overline{RS}$ is the base of triangle RST. The height of triangle RST is 4 units. What are the coordinates of point T?

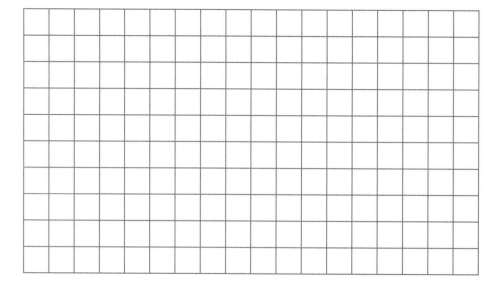

Name: _____   Date: _____

Find the area of each triangle.

6.

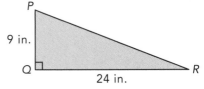

7.

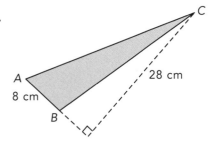

The area of each triangle is 60 square inches. Find the measure of *x*.

8.

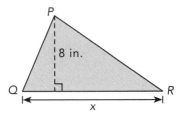

9.

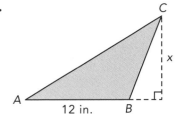

Find the area of each polygon.

10. *DEFG* is a parallelogram.

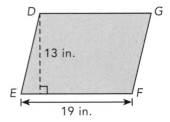

11. *HJKL* is a trapezoid.

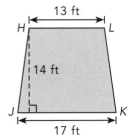

12. Find the area of the regular pentagon.

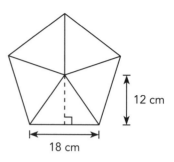

12 cm

18 cm

13. Find the area of the regular hexagon.

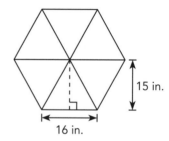

15 in.

16 in.

Find the circumference of each circle.

14. Use $\frac{22}{7}$ as an approximation for π.

21 in.

15. Use 3.14 as an approximation for π.

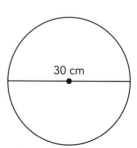

30 cm

Name: _____   Date: _____

Find the perimeter of each figure.

16. Use $\frac{22}{7}$ as an approximation for π.

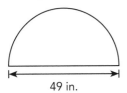

49 in.

17. Use 3.14 as an approximation for π.

20 in.

Find the area of each figure. Use 3.14 as an approximation for π.

18.

8 in.

19.

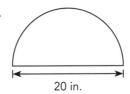

20 in.

Find the area of each figure. Use $\frac{22}{7}$ as an approximation for π.

20.

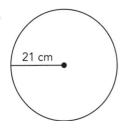

21 cm

21.

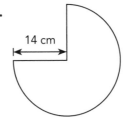

14 cm

Solve. Show your work.

22. A tube has a circular base with a radius of 6 centimeters. Find the area of the circular base. Use 3.14 as an approximation for π.

23. The opening of a tunnel is in the shape of a semicircle. The area of the semicircle is 77 square feet. Find its diameter. Use $\frac{22}{7}$ as an approximation for π.

24. The circumference of a circular hoop is 132 inches. Find its radius. Use $\frac{22}{7}$ as an approximation for π.

25. Faye has x yards of ribbon. Faye's ribbon is 4 times as long as Janelle's ribbon. If Janelle has 12 yards of ribbon, write and solve an equation to find the length of Faye's ribbon.

26. Mrs. Lim is y years old. She was 25 years old when her son was born. Their total age in 12 years' time will be n years.

a) Express n in terms of y.

b) Find n when $y = 38$.

27. Mick and LaToya have some shirts. The ratio of the number of shirts Mick has to the number of shirts LaToya has is 3 : 8. If they have a total of k shirts, how many fewer shirts does Mick have than LaToya?

28. A square tray has a side length of $9p$ inches. The perimeter of a rectangular tray is $\frac{1}{3}$ the perimeter of the square tray. If the width of the rectangular tray is $\frac{1}{2}$ its length, find the width of the rectangle in terms of p.

29. The hour hand of a clock is 8 centimeters long. How far does the tip of the hour hand travel in one day? Use 3.14 as an approximation for π.

30. The area of trapezoid *WXYZ* is 255 square inches. Find its height *h*.

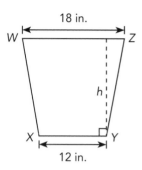

31. In rectangle *ABCD* shown, *AD* = 40 yards and *CD* = 30 yards. Find the area of the shaded regions.

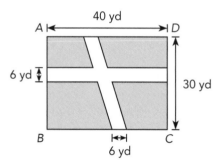

32. The figure shows rectangle *ABCD* overlapping with triangle *BCE*. The area of triangle *BCE* is 12 square centimeters larger than the area of rectangle *ABCD*. Find the length of $\overline{AB}$.

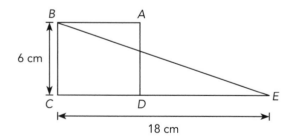

33. The figure shows two identical circles with centers O and R, and a rectangle

$OPQR$. If $PQ = 28$ inches, find the total area of the shaded regions. Use $\dfrac{22}{7}$ as an approximation for π.

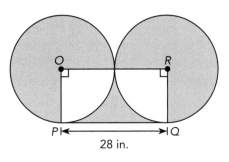

P $\longleftarrow$ Q

28 in.

34. If $BC = CD = DE$, what is the area of triangle ACD?

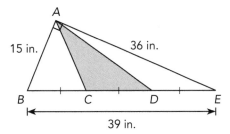

A

15 in.   36 in.

B   C   D   E

39 in.

35. Plot points *P* (2, 5), *Q* (−3, −3), and *R* (3, −3) on a coordinate plane.

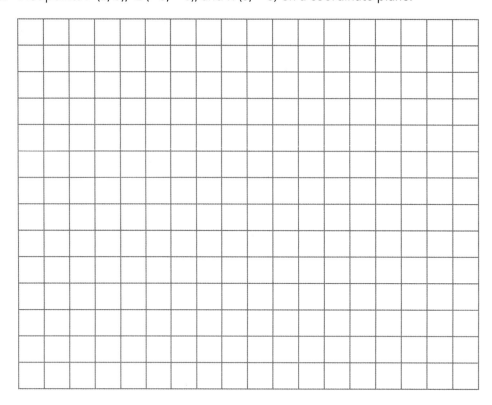

a)   Find the area of triangle *PQR*.

b)   Figure *PQRS* is a parallelogram. Point *S* has a positive *x*-coordinate and the same *y*-coordinate as point *P*. Plot point *S* on the coordinate plane and give its coordinates.

c)   Find the area of parallelogram *PQRS*.

d)   Triangle *TQR* is a right triangle, and its area is one-half the area of triangle *PQR*. Point *T* is above point *Q*. Plot point *T* on the coordinate plane and give its coordinates.

36. To print greeting cards, a company charges a flat fee of $10 plus $2 per card.
The total cost, C dollars, for printing n greeting cards is given by $C = 10 + 2n$.
The table shows the total cost for printing n greeting cards.

Number of Cards (n)	0	5	10	15		25
Total Cost (C dollars)	10	20			50	

a) Complete the table.
b) Graph the relationship between n and C. Use 1 unit on the horizontal axis to represent 5 cards and 1 unit on the vertical axis to represent $10.

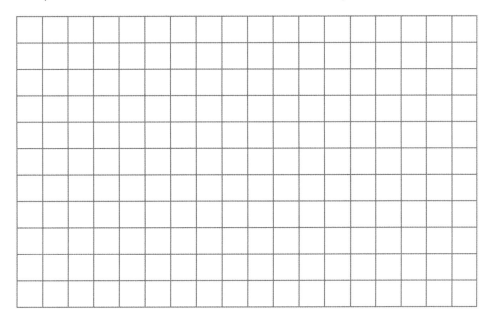

c) Olivia wants to print 30 greeting cards. What is her total cost?

d) Jaime wants to print 200 greeting cards. What is his total cost?

e) If Chloe has $50, how many greeting cards can she print? Express your answer in the form of an inequality, in terms of x.

f) Name the dependent and independent variables.

37. The maximum load of an elevator is 480 pounds. Assuming that the average mass of a student is 45 pounds, and *m* represents the number of students in the elevator, how many students can take the elevator at the same time?

   a) Express your answer in the form of an inequality in terms of *m*.

   b) Will the inequality in part **a)** be true if *m* = 11?

   c) Draw a number line to represent the solution of the inequality. Then state the maximum value of *m*.

38. The figure shown is made up of triangle *ABF* and rectangle *BCDE*. The area of the figure is 90 square feet. If *AB* = *BC* = *BF* = *FE*, find *AC*.

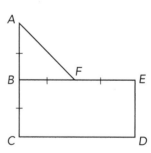

39. The figure shows a square, a semicircle, two identical quadrants, and a triangle. Find the total area of the shaded regions. Use $\frac{22}{7}$ as an approximation for π.

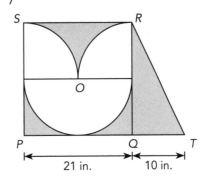

40. The figure shows three semicircles and a circle. If $AB = BC = CD = DE$, find the area of the shaded regions. Use $\frac{22}{7}$ as an approximation for π.

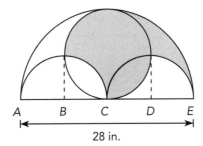

Name: _____   Date: _____

CHAPTER

Surface Area and Volume of Solids

Lesson 12.1   Nets of Solids

Name each solid. In each solid, identify a base and a face that is not base.

1.

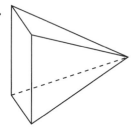

2.

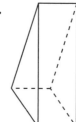

3.

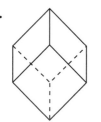

4.

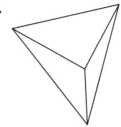

Name the solid that each net forms.

5.

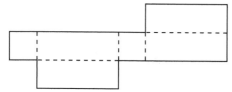

_____

6.

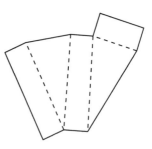

_____

7.

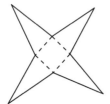

_____

8.

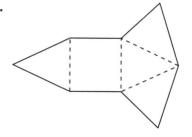

_____

Name: _____   Date: _____

Decide if each net will form a square pyramid.

9.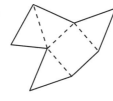

_____

10.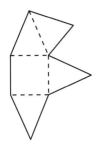

_____

11.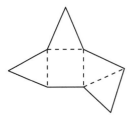

_____

12.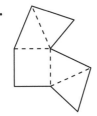

_____

13.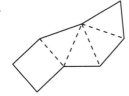

_____

14.

_____

Solve.

15. In Exercises **9** to **14**, you identified some possible nets for a square pyramid. There are other possible nets. Find five other possible nets.

Name the vertices that are not already labeled with a letter.

16.

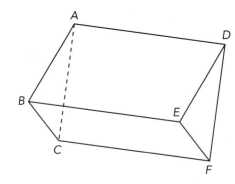

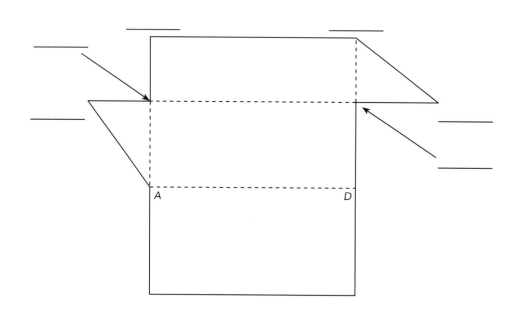

Lesson 12.2 Surface Area of Solids

Solve. Show your work.

1. A cube has edges measuring 9 inches each. Find the surface area of the cube.

2. A rectangular shipping container measures 20 feet by 8 feet by 6 feet. Find the
    surface area of the shipping container.

3. A triangular prism with its measurements is shown. Find the surface area of
    the prism.

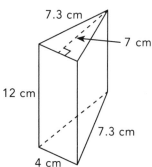

4. A wedge of cheese in the shape of a triangular prism is shown below. Find the
    surface area of the cheese.

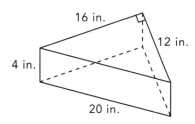

5. A block of wood is shaped like a prism with bases that are trapezoids. The block of wood has the measurements shown. What is the surface area of the block of wood?

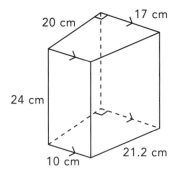

6. This solid consists of three identical trapezoidal faces and two equilateral triangular bases. The side lengths of the small triangular base is 5 inches and the side lengths of the large triangular base is 8 inches. The height of each trapezoidal face is 15 inches. Find the surface area of the solid.

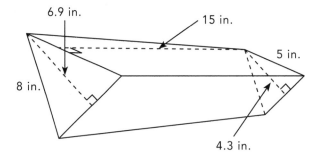

Name: _____ Date: _____

7. A community center is a prism with bases that are pentagons, and has the dimensions shown in the diagram.

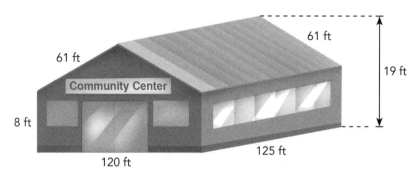

The external walls of the community center are to be painted. The doors and windows total 225 square feet and are not going to be painted. Find the total area of the walls that need to be painted.

8. A prism has m vertices. Write an expression for each of the following.
   a) the number of sides of each base

   b) the number of edges, and

   c) the number of faces.

Lesson 12.3   Volume of Prisms

Solve. Show your work.

1. A cube has edges measuring 8 inches each. Find the volume of the cube.

2. A box is shaped like a rectangular prism. The box is 3.5 feet long, 1.8 feet wide, and 2 feet high. Find the volume of the box.

3. Find the volume of the gift box.

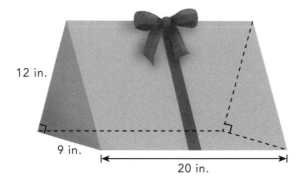

12 in.

9 in.

20 in.

4. The solid below is made of identical cubes. Each cube has an edge length of 3 inches. Find the volume of the solid.

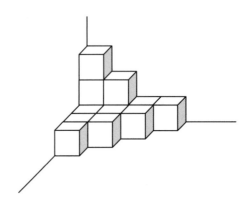

Tell whether slices parallel to each given slice will form uniform cross sections. If not, explain why not.

5.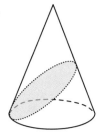

6.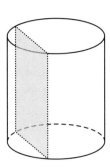

7.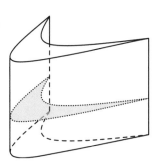

Solve. Show your work.

8. A cube has a volume of 512 cubic centimeters. Find the area of each face of the cube.

9. The volume of a rectangular prism with square bases is 5,880 cubic inches. It has a height of 30 inches. Find the side length of the square base.

10. A block of copper in the shape of a rectangular prism is 12 inches long, 6 inches wide, and 3 inches high. It is melted and recast into a cube. Find the edge length of the cube.

11. The bases of the prism shown are trapezoids. Find the volume of the prism.

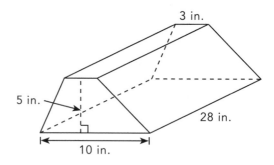

12. A cross section of the prism shown is parallel to a base. The area of the cross section is 78.5 square feet. The ratio of AB to BC is 5 : 4. The length of $\overline{AB}$ is 10 feet. Find the volume of the prism.

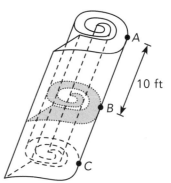

13. The solid is made by removing a smaller rectangular prism from a larger rectangular prism. Both prisms have square bases. The side length of the square base of the smaller prism is 4 centimeters. The side length of the square base of the larger prism is 12 centimeters. Find the volume of the solid.

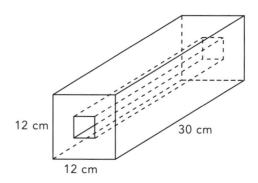

Name: _____   Date: _____

Lesson 12.4   Real-World Problems: Surface Area
and Volume

Solve. Show your work.

1. A nylon camping tent is shaped like a triangular prism. The triangular bases
   of the tent are isosceles triangles. The camping tent is closed at both ends
   and at the bottom. The surface area of the nylon is 136 square feet. Find the
   height h of the prism.

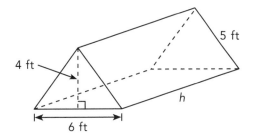

2. A water storage tank is shaped like a rectangular prism. The tank measures
   60 centimeters by 40 centimeters by 30 centimeters. The height of the water in
   the tank is 18 centimeters. How many cubic centimeters of water is needed to
   completely fill the tank?

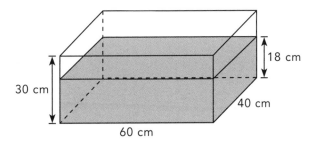

3. A brick wall shaped like a rectangular prism measures 450 centimeters long, 18 centimeters wide, and 108 centimeters high. The volume of one brick is 972 cubic centimeters. Find the number of bricks in the wall.

4. The volume of Box A is two times the volume of Box B. What is the height of Box B if it has a base area of 72 square inches?

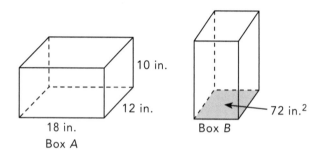

5. A solid block of wood has the measurements shown.
   a) Find the volume of the prism.

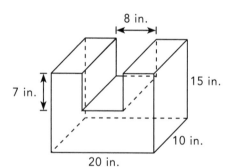

   b) Find the surface area of the prism.

Name: _____ Date: _____

6. A rectangular tank is filled with water to a height of 6 centimeters as shown. The ratio of the volume of water in the tank to the volume of water in a pail is 9 : 4. Assume that $\frac{4}{5}$ of the pail is filled with water.

a) Find the capacity of the pail.

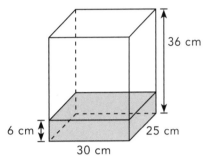

36 cm

6 cm

25 cm

30 cm

b) Find the minimum number of pails of water needed to fill the tank completely.

7. A swimming pool has bases that are trapezoids, and has the dimensions shown in the diagram. The surface area of the swimming pool is 3,222.5 square meters.

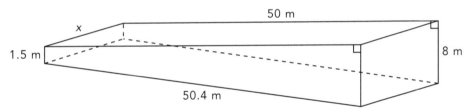

50 m

x

1.5 m

8 m

50.4 m

a) Find the measure of x.

b) Find the volume of the swimming pool.

8. A rectangular tank with a square base is $\frac{1}{4}$ full of water. The side length of the square base is 20 inches. When another 3,000 cubic inches of water is poured into the tank, it becomes $\frac{2}{3}$ full.

  a) Find the capacity of the tank.

  b) When the tank is $\frac{2}{3}$ full, what is the height of the water?

Name: _____   Date: _____

Solve. Show your work.

1. A rectangular piece of cardboard measuring 30 inches by 20 inches is made into an open box by first cutting an identical square from each corner, and then folding up the sides. The edge of each identical square is a whole number.

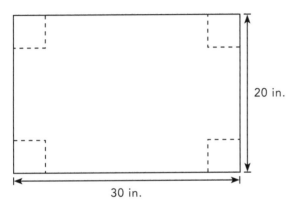

20 in.

30 in.

a) Find the maximum volume of the box. (Hint: Use a table to help you.)

b) Using the box with the maximum volume, what is the side length of each identical square?

2. The solid below is made of identical cubes. Each cube has an edge length of 3 inches.

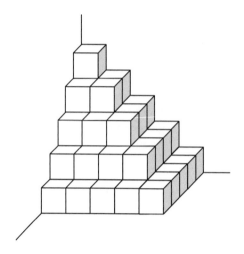

a) Find the volume of the solid.

b) Find the surface area of the solid.

Name: _____   Date: _____

Introduction to Statistics

Lesson 13.1   Collecting and Tabulating Data

Complete the table. Solve.

1. A car dealership conducted a survey among their customers. They asked their customers to state their favorite car between models A, B, C, and D.

    A tally chart was used to record their findings.

Model	Tally	Frequency
A	~~HHH~~ ~~HHH~~ //	
B	~~HHH~~ ~~HHH~~ /	
C	~~HHH~~ ////	
D	~~HHH~~ ///	

a)   How many customers took part in the survey?

b)   How many more customers prefer model A than model D?

c)   What percent of the customers surveyed stated model A as their favorite?

Name: _____   Date: _____

2. Some students were asked to name their favorite Olympic sport.
   The following responses were the choices provided:

   (a) basketball   (b) soccer   (c) hockey   (d) swimming

Sport	Tally	Frequency
Basketball	HHT HHT	
Soccer	HHT /	
Hockey	HHT	
Swimming	HHT HHT HHT	

a)   How many students were questioned?

b)   How many students named swimming or hockey as their favorite
     Olympic sport?

c)   What percent of the students named soccer as their favorite
     Olympic sport?

Name: _____   Date: _____

Tabulate the data. Solve. Show your work.

3. Mr. Rickman wanted to find out how many hours in a day his students spend surfing the Internet. The average number of hours reported by each student is shown.

Number of Hours

1	3	3	4	2	0	2	2	2
2	3	5	4	3	5	3	3	3
6	6	3	5	6	3	4	5	6

a) Arrange the numbers in ascending order.

b) Complete the frequency table.

Number of Hours	Tally	Frequency
0–2		
3–4		
5–6		

c) How many students surf the Internet for more than 2 hours each day?

d) How many students surf the Internet for less than 5 hours each day?

4. Candice conducted a survey among 30 families in her neighborhood. She asked them the number of pets in their household. These are the data she collected:

Number of Pets

2	1	3	2	2	0	3	1	0	4
0	2	2	1	3	2	4	0	1	1
3	2	2	1	1	1	0	0	3	2

a) Arrange the numbers in ascending order.

b) Complete the frequency table.

Number of Pets	Tally	Frequency
0–1		
2–3		
4–5		

c) How many families own at least 2 pets?

d) What percent of the families own 4 to 5 pets?

Lesson 13.2   Dot Plots

A group of students were asked the number of hours they read for pleasure each day. The number of hours is shown. Use the data to answer questions 1 to 4.

1	2	3	4	5	0	1	4	2	2
5	4	3	3	2	3	3	2	3	4

1. Represent the data with a dot plot. Give the dot plot a title.

2. How many observations are there?

3. What conclusions can you draw with regard to the number of hours the students read for pleasure?

4. What percent of the students spend 5 hours reading for pleasure?

A group of students were asked the number of mobile phone charms they own. The number of charms is shown. Use the data to answer questions 5 to 8.

3	2	3	1	1	1	0	1	0
4	0	3	0	2	1	2	1	2
2	0	1	1	1	0	2	0	0

5. Represent the data with a dot plot. Give the dot plot a title.

6. How many observations are there?

7. What conclusions can you draw with regard to the number of charms the students own?

8. What percent of the students own more than 2 charms? Round your answer to the nearest percent.

Name: _____   Date: _____

The dot plot shows the number of movies a group of students watched in the last three months. Use the dot plot to answer questions 9 to 12.

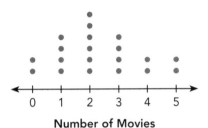

Number of Movies

9. Find the number of students surveyed.

10. What conclusion can you draw with regards to the number of movies the students watched?

11. What percent of the students watched at least 3 movies?

12. Briefly describe the distribution of the data.

Name: _____   Date: _____

The dot plot shows the math quiz scores of a group of students. The maximum score is 10 points. Use the dot plot to answer questions 13 to 16.

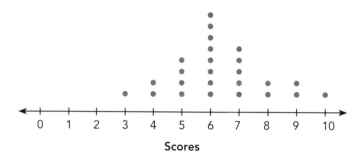

Scores

13. How many students took the quiz?

14. What percent of the students scored at least 8 points?

15. What conclusion can you draw with regards to the points?

16. Briefly describe the distribution of the data.

**The dot plot shows the number of board games owned by some children.
Use the dot plot to answer questions 17 to 19.**

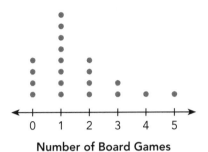

Number of Board Games

17. How many observations are there?

18. What percent of the children have less than 2 board games?

19. A few more children were surveyed and all of them have less than
2 board games. Of all of the children surveyed, $\frac{5}{7}$ of them have less than
2 board games. How many more children were surveyed?

Lesson 13.3   Histograms

Draw a histogram for each set of data. Include a title.

1. The table shows the number of goals scored by a hockey player during one season.

Number of Goals	0–1	2–3	4–5	6–7
Frequency	9	8	3	1

2. The table shows the number of spoons in the kitchens of 45 households.

Number of Spoons	0–3	4–7	8–11	12–15	16–19
Frequency	5	15	20	2	3

3. The table shows the number of computers in 16 laboratories in a university.

Number of Computers	0–2	3–5	6–8	9–11
Frequency	9	6	0	1

4. The table shows the number of buttons on 16 jackets.

Number of Buttons	5–10	11–16	17–22	23–28
Frequency	2	7	6	1

The times taken by 30 students to complete a mathematics assignment are shown in the table. The times were rounded to the nearest minute. Use the data to answer questions 5 to 7.

Time (*t* minutes)	21–25	26–30	31–35	36–40	41–45
Frequency	2	6	10	8	*p*

5. Find the value of *p*.

6. Draw a histogram to represent the data. Include a title. Briefly describe the data.

7. What percent of students took at least 36 minutes to complete their assignment?

The histogram shows the distances between a group of students' homes and the school. The distances are rounded to the nearest mile. Use the histogram to answer questions 8 to 10.

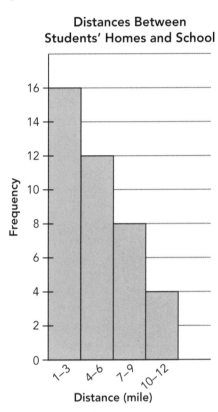

Distances Between
Students' Homes and School

8. How many observations are there?

9. What percent of the students live at most 6 miles from the school?

10. Briefly describe the data.

Name: _____   Date: _____

The histogram shows the mobile phone bills of a group of 30 students in one month. The amount of money is rounded to the nearest dollar. Use the histogram to answer questions 11 to 13.

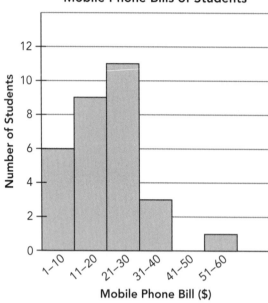

Mobile Phone Bills of Students

11. How many students have a mobile phone bill greater than $30?

12. What fraction of the students has mobile phone bills of at least $21?

13. Briefly describe the data. Explain whether the histogram shows any outlier of the data set.

Name: _____ Date: _____

The data shows the parking durations, in minutes, of 20 cars in a car park.
Use the data to answer questions 14 to 17.

25	38	105	75	65	95	28	40	80	115
70	110	95	45	30	90	86	80	100	62

14. Complete the frequency table to show this data.

Duration (min)	0–29	30–59	60–89	90–119
Frequency				

15. Draw a histogram using the interval. Include a title.

16. What percent of the parking durations are greater than 59 minutes?

17. Briefly describe the data.

Name: _____   Date: _____

The heights of 50 plants of one species are shown in the table. The heights are rounded to the nearest centimeter. Use the data to answer questions 18 to 22.

Height (cm)	1–10	11–20	21–30	31–40	41–50	51–60	61–70
Number of Plants	1	2	x	6	12	y	10

The heights of 36 plants are at least 41 centimeters high.

18. Find the values of x and y.

19. Draw a histogram using the interval. Include a title.

20. The height of a healthy plant should be greater than 30 centimeters. What percent of the plants are in poor health?

21. If the plants were to be categorized as follows:
poor growth: heights between 1 centimeter and 30 centimeters,
normal growth: heights between 31 centimeters and 50 centimeters, and
excellent growth: heights between 51 centimeters and 70 centimeters,
draw a histogram for the above data using the new categories.

22. Compare the two histograms. Describe a situation when one histogram would be more useful than the other.

CHAPTER

The numbers of years some teachers have been employed are shown in the table. Use the data to answer questions 1 to 2.

Number of Years Employed (yr)	0–1	2–3	4–5	6–9
Frequency	14	13	8	5

A histogram was drawn to represent the data.

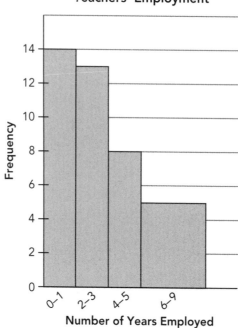

Teachers' Employment

1. Explain why the histogram above is not appropriate.

2. Draw a histogram to correctly represent the data. Include a title.

CHAPTER

Measures of Central Tendency

Lesson 14.1   Mean

Find the mean of each data set.

1. 9, 10, 11, 16, 12, 12, 14

2. 20, 22, 21, 23, 25, 24, 26, 28, 27

3. 17.4 mm, 20.3 mm, 84.1 mm, 31.2 mm, 53.7 mm, 11.7 mm

Solve. Show your work.

4. The heights of five peacocks are 3.8 feet, 5.2 feet, 4.8 feet, 5.0 feet, and 4.6 feet. Find the mean height of these five peacocks.

5. The amount of time eight paper airplanes stayed in the air are 11.3 seconds, 15.2 seconds, 12.0 seconds, 13.6 seconds, 12.8 seconds, 10.9 seconds, 14.2 seconds, and 14.0 seconds. Find the mean time these eight paper airplanes stayed in the air.

Name: _____   Date: _____

Use the data in the table to answer the question.

The table shows the number of pins that fell in the first five frames of a bowling game.

Bowling Score

Frame Number	1	2	3	4	5
Number of Pins	9	5	7	9	5

6. Find the mean number of pins that fell in the first five frames of the bowling game.

The dot plot shows the number of headbands owned by a group of girls. Use the dot plot to answer questions 7 to 9.

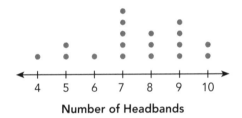

Number of Headbands

7. How many girls are in the group?

8. Find the total number of headbands.

9. Find the mean number of headbands each girl owns.

Solve. Show your work.

10. The mean of eight numbers is 83. The mean of another four numbers is 14. Find the mean of the combined set of numbers.

11. The mean number of pillows in nine boxes is 13. There are 12, 10, 15, 12, 13, 15, 11, and 13 pillows in eight boxes. Find the number of pillows in the last box.

12. The mean height of eight plants is 18 inches. The heights of seven plants are 12 inches, 13 inches, 15 inches, 15 inches, 17 inches, 23 inches, and 24 inches. Find the height of the eighth plant.

13. The mean of six numbers is 41. If one number is removed, the mean of the five numbers is 46. Find the unknown number.

14. The mean of seven numbers is 21. Five of the numbers are 18, 23, 21, 17, and 19. One of the remaining numbers is $\frac{3}{4}$ of the other remaining number. Find the two unknown numbers.

15. The mean of nine numbers is 6. If two of the nine numbers are removed, the mean of the seven numbers is still 6. One of the numbers is 4 more than the other number. Find the greater unknown number.

16. The mean of a set of twelve numbers is 5.5. The mean of another set of eight numbers is k. The mean of the combined set of twenty numbers is 8.5. Find the value of k.

Lesson 14.2   Median

Find the median of each data set.

1. 5, 7, 9, 6, 3, 9, 11

2. 25, 27, 19, 18, 28, 22, 25, 30, 20

3. 3.5, 4.8, 2.6, 5.6, 8.4, 6.5, 2.4, 9.5

4. $6\frac{1}{4}, 3\frac{3}{4}, 4\frac{1}{4}, 3\frac{1}{2}, 5\frac{7}{12}, 4\frac{3}{4}$

Solve. Show your work.

5. The shop has sweatshirts for sale in the following sizes 8, 10, 8, 12, 14, 10, 14, 16, and 10. Find the median size of sweatshirts for sale.

6. The number of fish caught by ten competitors in a fishing competition is 7, 5, 4, 6, 5, 6, 5, 3, 8, and 3. Find the median number of fish caught.

The dot plot shows the number of countries visited by each student in a class. Each dot represents one student. Use the data in the dot plot to answer questions 7 to 10.

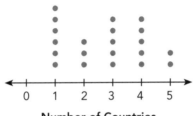

Number of Countries

7. Find the total number of students.

8. What is the mean number of countries visited by each student? Round your answer to the nearest tenth.

9. Find the median number of countries visited.

10. Which of the two measures of central tendency, the mean or the median, better describes the data set? Justify your answer.

Solve. Show your work.

11. The median of a set of six numbers is 47. The six numbers are 13, 43, 34, 52, 64, and q. Find the value of q.

12. The median of a set of twelve numbers is 27. The twelve numbers are 32, 30, 20, 30, 28, 22, 29, 25, 32, 24, 23, and b. Find the value of b.

13. The data set shows a set of numbers.

5, 2, 8, 10, 9, 4, 9, 4, x, y

The mean and median of the set of numbers is 7. The value of x is less than the value of y. Find the values of x and y.

14. The median of a set of numbers is x. There are at least three numbers in the set. Write an algebraic expression, in terms of x, to represent the median of the new set of numbers obtained by

a)   adding $\dfrac{1}{8}$ to every number in the set.

b)   subtracting $9\dfrac{1}{4}$ from every number in the set.

c)   multiplying -5.8 to every number in the set and then adding 3 to the resulting numbers.

d)   dividing every number in the set by 0.5 and then subtracting 1 from the resulting numbers.

e)   adding 7.2 to the greatest number in the set.

f)   subtracting 4.2 from the least number in the set.

Lesson 14.3   Mode

Find the mode or modes of each data set.

1. 3, 4, 7, 4, 5, 5, 4, 3, 4

2. 12, 13, 15, 12, 15, 16, 12, 17, 12

3. 8.1, 7.7, 5.8, 7.7, 9.3, 5.3, 4.8, 9.3, 8.1, 9.3, 6.4, 7.7

Find the mode.

4. The dot plot shows the erasers in some school boxes. Each dot represents one school box. Find the mode.

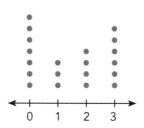

Number of Erasers

5. The table shows the favorite fruits of a group of students. Find the mode.

Favorite Fruits of Students

Fruit	Number of Students
Peach	7
Grapes	10
Apples	6
Pears	15
Oranges	22

The data set shows the number of apples on each tree on a plot of land.
Use the data to answer questions 6 to 9.

102	101	102	102	103	102	101
101	104	102	101	102	103	101
102	105	104	102	103	104	101

6. Make a dot plot to show the data. Give the dot plot a title.

7. What is the mean number of apples? Round your answer to the nearest whole number.

8. What is the median number of apples?

9. What is the modal number of apples?

Name: _____   Date: _____

Solve. Show your work.

10. The ages of the children in a choir are listed in the data set below.
The minimum age to participate in the choir is 7 years old. The maximum
age is 12 years old.

11, 8, 10, 8, 12, 11, 12, 9, 9, 10, 12, 10, 10, 8, 10, 10, 11, 9, 11, 12, 11, 8, 11, 9, 12,
10, 9, 11, x

a) If there are two modes, what are the possible values of x?

b) If there is exactly one mode, write a possible value for x, and the mode.

11. The table below shows the number of light bulbs that need to be replaced on each
floor of a building in a month. The total number of floors in the building is 30.

Number of Light Bulbs Needed

Number of Light Bulbs	0	1	2	3	4	5	6
Number of Floors	1	4	6	x	8	y	2

a) The mode for this set of data is 4. The value of x is greater than the value of y.
Find the greatest possible value of x.

b) Find the median number of light bulbs that need to be replaced. Use the values
of x and y from question **a)**.

c) Find the mean number of light bulbs that need to be replaced. Use the values
of x and y from question **a)**. Round your answer to the nearest whole number.

Lesson 14.4 Real-World Problems: Mean, Median, and Mode

Find the mean, median, and mode.

1. The amount of honey harvested, in gallons, from a hive for 15 years is 6, 3, 6, 6, 5, 6, 7, 7, 3, 4, 7, 5, 6, 4, and 7. Find the mean, median, and mode. Round your answers to the nearest tenth of a gallon.

Use the data in the table to answer each question.

The table shows the number of windows in 50 houses.

Number of Windows in 50 Houses

Number of Windows	3	4	5	6	7	8
Number of Houses	3	6	14	15	7	5

2. Find the mean, median, and mode.

3. Which measure of central tendency best describes the data set? Justify your answer.

Name: _____   Date: _____

Solve. Show your work.

The data set shows the number of hours students spent online shopping during one week.

0, 0, 0, 1, 1, 1, 2, 2, 2, 2, 2, 2, 2, 3, 3, 3, 3, 3, 2, 2

4. Find the mean, median, and mode.

5. What is the least whole number you should include in the data set if you want the mean to be greater than the median?

Use the data in the dot plot to answer the question.

The dot plot shows a town's daily low temperature, in degrees Celsius, for 24 days.

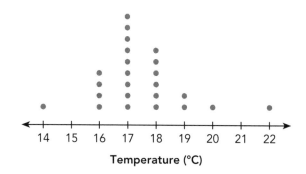

Temperature (°C)

6. Briefly describe the data distribution and relate the measure of center to the shape of the dot plot shown.

Name: _____   Date: _____

Use the data in the dot plot to answer each question.

The dot plot shows the number of public holidays in some countries. Each dot represents 1 country.

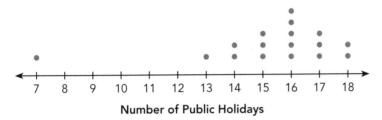

Number of Public Holidays

7. Find the mean, median, and mode. Round your answers to the nearest whole number.

8. Give a reason why the mean is less than the median.

9. Which measure of central tendency best describes the data set? Explain.

10. Relate the measures of center to the shape of the data distribution.

Name: _____   Date: _____

Make a dot plot to show the data. Use your dot plot to answer each question.

The lengths of 20 leaves were correctly measured to the nearest centimeter.
The following information is known about the results.

The number of leaves that measure 2 centimeters is two times the number of leaves measuring 4 centimeters, and 8 centimeters. It is also half the number of leaves measuring 3 centimeters.

The ratio of the number of leaves measuring 5 centimeters to the number of leaves measuring 6 centimeters, to the number of leaves measuring 7 centimeters is 1 : 2 : 1.

There are 2 more leaves measuring 6 centimeters than leaves measuring 3 centimeters.

11. Make a dot plot to show the data. Give the dot plot a title.

12. Briefly describe the data distribution and relate the measure of center to the shape of the dot plot shown.

CHAPTER

 **Brain @ Work**

Find the values of the missing numbers.

1. The number of members in a society for each of four months is 102, 104, 75, and 70, as shown in the table. The mean number of members during a six month period is $92\frac{1}{6}$.

Month	Jan	Feb	Mar	Apr	May	Jun
Number of Members	102	104	?	75	70	?

If one of the missing numbers in the table drops by 25%, the mean number of members becomes $87\frac{5}{6}$. What are the two missing numbers?

Cumulative Practice
for Chapters 12 to 14

Match each of the solid figures to its nets.

1.
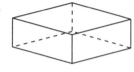

2.
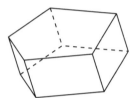

3.
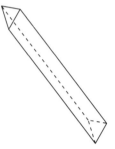

a)
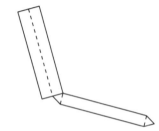

b)
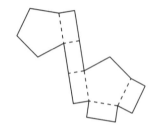

c)
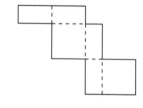

Find the surface area and volume of each prism.

4.
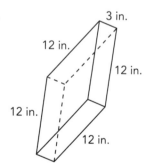

3 in.
12 in.
12 in.
12 in.
12 in.

5.
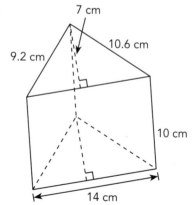

7 cm
10.6 cm
9.2 cm
10 cm
14 cm

Name: _____   Date: _____

 The volume of each rectangular prism is 232 cubic meters.
The rectangular prisms have square bases. Find the lengths of an
edge of one of the square bases. Round your answers to the nearest
tenth of a meter.

6.

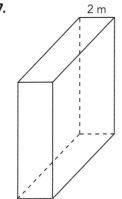

15 m

7.

2 m

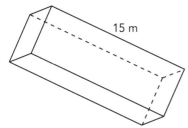

Solve. Show your work.

8. The solid below is made up of identical cubes. The edge length of each cube
is 4 inches. Find the volume of the solid.

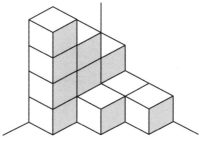

9. The solid below is made up of identical cubes. The volume of the solid
is 243 cubic inches. Find the surface area of the solid.

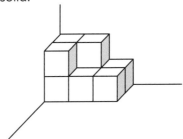

Solve. Show your work.

10. The data set shows the ages of eight students.
    10 yr, 15 yr, 16 yr, 8 yr, 12 yr, 15 yr, 14 yr, 10 yr
    Find the mean, and median ages of these eight students.

11. The data set shows the times of ten runners in a race.
    56.0 s, 55.5 s, 55.4 s, 55.9 s, 55.7 s, 56.3 s, 56.2 s, 55.9 s, 55.6 s, 56.5 s
    Find the mean, and median times of these ten runners.

12. The data set shows the duration of twelve songs, in minutes, on an album.
    $4, 3\frac{1}{3}, 4\frac{1}{3}, 2\frac{8}{15}, 5\frac{2}{3}, 3\frac{8}{15}, 2, 6, 1\frac{4}{15}, 5\frac{2}{3}, 5\frac{4}{5}, 5\frac{11}{30}$
    Find the mean, and median durations of these twelve songs.

Name: _____ Date: _____

The weights, in ounces, of 30 peaches are recorded below. Use the data to answer questions 13 to 15.

4.5	5.0	4.0	6.0	4.5	5.0	5.0	6.0	7.0	5.5
5.0	6.5	5.5	5.5	5.0	4.0	5.5	5.5	6.0	5.5
4.5	3.5	4.5	4.0	3.5	5.0	6.5	4.5	6.0	6.5

13. Represent the set of data with a dot plot. Give the dot plot a title.

14. Group the data into suitable intervals and tabulate them.

15. Draw a histogram using the interval. Include a title. Briefly describe the data.

Describe the data.

16. The histogram shows the duration, in minutes, of people waiting for a taxi.
The durations were recorded to the nearest minute.
Briefly describe the data.

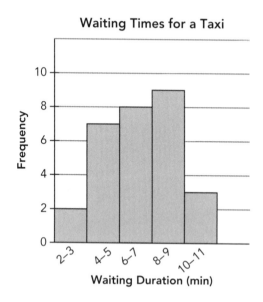

The data set shows the vertical jump height, in inches, of 24 students.
Use the data to answer questions 17 to 18.

| 35 | 34 | 37 | 38 | 36 | 33 | 34 | 38 | 36 | 33 | 35 | 34 |
| 34 | 36 | 35 | 33 | 39 | 34 | 32 | 35 | 37 | 38 | 36 | 39 |

17. Represent the set of data with a dot plot. Give the dot plot a title.

18. Find the mean, median, and mode of the data set. Round your answers to the nearest whole number.

The data set shows the number of muffins a bakery makes each day for a month. Use the data to answer questions 19 to 20.

101	100	102	101	100	105	100	101	102	101
103	101	102	103	100	102	101	104	103	100
101	102	101	104	102	101	103	102	101	102

19. Represent the set of data with a dot plot. Give the dot plot a title.

20. Find the mean, median, and mode of the data set. Round your answers to the nearest number of muffins.

Solve. Show your work.

21. The surface area of the square pyramid is 576 square inches. The square pyramid has congruent triangular faces. The ratio of the area of each triangular face to the area of the square base is 3 : 4. Find the length of an edge of the square base.

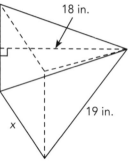

18 in.

19 in.

x

22. A rectangular glass container is 160 centimeters long, 80 centimeters wide, and x centimeters high. The height of the water in the rectangular container was $\frac{5}{8}$ the height of the container. Edward poured out 156,000 cubic centimeters of water from the container. The height of the water is now $\frac{1}{4}$ the height of the container.

   a) Find the height of the rectangular container.

   b) Find the amount of glass, in square centimeters, used to make the bottom and sides of the container.

Name: _____ Date: _____

23. The table shows the number of telephones in 25 offices.

Number of Telephones	12–15	16–19	20–23	24–27	28–31
Number of Offices	3	a	8	5	1

a) Find the value of a.

b) Draw a histogram to represent the data. Include a title. Briefly describe the data.

c) What percent of the offices had more than 23 telephones?

d) What percent of the offices had less than 20 telephones?

Make a dot plot to show the data. Use your dot plot to answer each question.

24. The table shows the time taken, in seconds, by 52 students to solve a puzzle.

Time (s)	21	22	23	24	25	26
Number of Students	2	q	8	14	p	8

The total number of students that took at least 24 seconds to solve the puzzle is 37.

a) Find the values of p and q. Then represent this set of data with a dot plot. Give the dot plot a title.

b) Find the mean of the data set. Round your answers to the nearest second.

c) Another school tested 30 more students, and the mean time is 25 seconds. If the two data sets are combined, find the mean time of the combined data set. Round your answer to the nearest tenth of a second.

Answers

Chapter 8

Lesson 8.1

1. If $x = 4$, $4 + 8 = 12$.
   If $x = 6$, $6 + 8 = 14$.
   So, $x = 6$.
2. If $y = 10$, $10 + 6 = 16$.
   If $y = 14$, $14 + 6 = 20$.
   So, $y = 14$.
3. If $p = 14$, $14 - 9 = 5$.
   If $p = 16$, $16 - 9 = 7$.
   So, $p = 16$.
4. If $k = 30$, $30 - 15 = 15$.
   If $k = 35$, $35 - 15 = 20$.
   So, $k = 35$.
5. If $w = 12$, $6 \cdot 12 = 72$.
   So, $w = 12$.
6. If $q = 4$, $15 \cdot 4 = 60$.
   So, $q = 4$.
7. If $e = 56$, $\frac{1}{8} \cdot 56 = 7$.
   So, $e = 56$.
8. If $g = 120$, $\frac{1}{10} \cdot 120 = 12$.
   So, $g = 120$.
9. $a + 14 - 14 = 20 - 14$
   $a = 6$
10. $b + 18 - 18 = 34 - 18$
    $b = 16$
11. $18 + 12 = s - 12 + 12$
    $s = 30$
12. $h - 15 + 15 = 9 + 15$
    $h = 24$
13. $7k \div 7 = 84 \div 7$
    $k = 12$
14. $\frac{m}{6} \cdot 6 = 16 \cdot 6$
    $m = 96$
15. $x + \frac{1}{6} - \frac{1}{6} = \frac{5}{6} - \frac{1}{6}$
    $x = \frac{4}{6} = \frac{2}{3}$
16. $y - \frac{2}{5} + \frac{2}{5} = \frac{3}{5} + \frac{2}{5}$
    $y = \frac{5}{5} = 1$
17. $8k \div 8 = \frac{4}{9} \div 8$
    $k = \frac{1}{18}$
18. $10g \div 10 = \frac{4}{6} \div 10$
    $g = \frac{1}{15}$

19. $\frac{3}{5} \cdot \frac{5}{3}p = \frac{1}{10} \cdot \frac{5}{3}$
    $p = \frac{1}{2}$
20. $\frac{3}{2} \cdot \frac{2}{3}w = \frac{5}{6} \cdot \frac{3}{2}$
    $w = 1\frac{1}{4}$
21. $x + 1.8 - 1.8 = 3.4 - 1.8$
    $x = 1.6$
22. $p + 6.3 - 6.3 = 9.1 - 6.3$
    $p = 2.8$
23. $y - 3.5 + 3.5 = 2.9 + 3.5$
    $y = 6.4$
24. $k - 8.5 + 8.5 = 2.7 + 8.5$
    $k = 11.2$
25. $3x + 2.5 - 2.5 = 6.1 - 2.5$
    $3x = 3.6$
    $3x \div 3 = 3.6 \div 3$
    $x = 1.2$
26. $4y - 6.2 + 6.2 = 13 + 6.2$
    $4y = 19.2$
    $4y \div 4 = 19.2 \div 4$
    $y = 4.8$
27. $k = 40 \div 3.2$
    $k = 12.5$
28. $p = 36 \div 2.4$
    $p = 15$
29. $w + \frac{2}{3} - \frac{2}{3} = 2\frac{5}{6} - \frac{2}{3}$
    $w = 2\frac{1}{6}$
30. $d - \frac{2}{5} + \frac{2}{5} = 1\frac{3}{10} + \frac{2}{5}$
    $d = 1\frac{7}{10}$
31. $\frac{3y}{4} \cdot 4 = 15 \cdot 4$
    $3y = 60$
    $y = 20$
32. $\frac{7}{3} \cdot \frac{3}{7}k = \frac{7}{3} \cdot 6$
    $k = 14$
33. One possible solution:
    If $a = 3$, $b = 2$, $c = 20$, then the equation is
    $3x + 2 = 20$
    $3x + 2 - 2 = 20 - 2$
    $3x = 18$
    $x = 6$

Lesson 8.2

1. a) $w = 4z$
   b) Independent variable: z;
       dependent variable: w
2. a) $d = 2g - 1.5$
   b) Independent variable: g;
       dependent variable: d

3. a) $x = 4 - 7y$

   b) Independent variable: y; dependent variable: x

4. a) $c = \dfrac{b}{3}$

   b) Independent variable: b; dependent variable: c

5. a) $g = k - 20$

   b) 80; 100; 120; 130

6. a) $b = 4p + 10$

   b) 18; 26; 34; 42

7. a) $w = 8c$ or $c = \dfrac{w}{8}$

   b) 16; 24; 32; 40; 48; 56

   c)

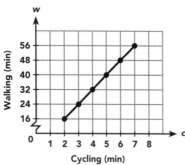

   d) $5\dfrac{1}{2}$ minutes

8. a) $h = 2p + 3$

   b) 5; 7; 9; 11; 13

   c)

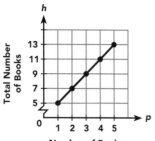

   d) Rachel reads 6 books.

9. a) $y = 80 - 5x$

   b) 75; 70; 65; 60; 55; 50

   c)

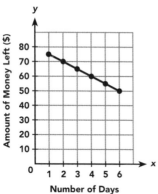

Lesson 8.3

1. $g \le 55$

2. $q \ge 28$

3. $p > 15$

4. $y < 20$

5.

6.

7.

8. $a > 14$

9. $a \ge 11$

10. $a < 14$

11. $a \le 15$

12.

Three possible integers are 5, 6, and 7.

13.

Three possible integers are 8, 9, and 10.

14.

Three possible integers are 3, 4, and 5.

15.

Three possible integers are 1, 2, and 3.

16. a) $x > 8.5$

   b) No. x is more than 8.5.

   c)

The least possible distance is 9 miles.

17. a) $y \le 20$

   b) Yes. 18 is less than 20.

   c)

The maximum value of y is 20.

18.

19.

20.

21.

Lesson 8.4

1. $2x = 48$
    $x = 24$
    The number is 24.

2. $b - 28 = 35$
    $b = 35 + 28$
    $b = 63$
    There were 63 novels in the school library at first.

3. $\frac{3}{5}s = 24$
    $\frac{1}{5}s = 8$
    $s = 40$
    There are 40 participants in the swimming class.

4. $5h \le 42$
    $h \le 8.4$
    $h = 8$
    Claire completes 8 laps.

5. $8c \le 60$
    $c \le 7.5$
    $c = 7$
    The box can hold 7 bundles of comic books.

6. $3y - 8 = 16$
    $3y = 16 + 8$
    $y = 8$
    The number is 8.

7. $4k - k = 117$
    $3k = 117$
    $k = 39$
    The smaller number is 39.

8. In 4 years' time, Shauna will be $(d + 4)$ years old and Jason will be $(3d + 4)$ years old.
    $d + 4 + 3d + 4 = 56$
    $4d + 8 = 56$
    $4d = 48$
    $d = 12$ (Shauna)
    $3d = 3 \cdot 12 = 36$ (Jason)
    Shauna is 12 years old and Jason is 36 years old.

9. If x dollars is the price of each hat, then each T-shirt costs $(x + 3)$ dollars.
    $6x + 7(x + 3) = 86$
    $6x + 7x + 21 = 86$
    $13x + 21 - 21 = 86 - 21$
    $13x = 65$
    $x = 5$ (hat)
    $x + 3 = 8$ (T-shirt)
    Mrs. Jones pays $5 for a hat and $8 for a T-shirt.

10. Let y the number of teachers needed.
    $15y \ge 100$
    $y \ge 6\frac{2}{3}$
    $y = 7$
    7 teachers are needed.

11. Let x be the number of Karen's lawn chairs.
    $x + 2x + x + 3 = 31$
    $4x + 3 = 31$
    $4x = 28$
    $x = 7$
    Karen has 7 lawn chairs.

12. Let y be the number of dimes Jared has.
    $0.1y + 0.25(y + 8) = 5.5$
    $0.1y + 0.25y + 2 = 5.5$
    $0.35y + 2 = 5.5$
    $0.35y = 3.5$
    $y = 10$
    Jared has 10 dimes.

Brain @ Work

1. If c is Montell's present age, then his mother's present age is $(c + 30)$.
    In 5 years, Montell will be $(c + 5)$ years old and his mother will be $(c + 35)$ years old.
    $3(c + 5) = c + 35$
    $3c + 15 = c + 35$
    $3c + 15 - 15 = c + 35 - 15$
    $3c = c + 20$
    $3c - c = c - c + 20$
    $2c = 20$
    $c = 10$ (Montell)
    $10 + 30 = 40$
    Montell's mother is 40 years old now.

2. If w inches is the width, then the length is $2w$ inches.
    The perimeter of the rectangle is $(w + 2w + w + 2w) = 6w$ inches.
    $6w < 74$
    $w < 12\frac{1}{3}$
    Its maximum width is 12 inches.

Chapter 9

Lesson 9.1

1. $P\,(-4, 2)$ $Q\,(-3, 0)$
    $R\,(-4, -1)$ $S\,(-3, -2)$
    $T\,(0, -3)$ $U\,(7, -2)$
    $V\,(2, 2)$ $W\,(4, 1)$

2.

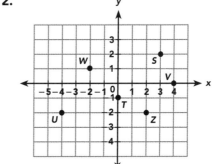

Quadrant I: Point *S*
Quadrant II: Point *W*
Quadrant III: Point *U*
Quadrant IV: Point *Z*
Point *T* lies on the *y*-axis between
Quadrant III and Quadrant IV.
Point *V* lies on the *x*-axis between Quadrant I
and Quadrant IV.

3. (−3, 9) **4.** (7, 4)
5. (5, −6) **6.** (−8, −2)
7. (3, −9) **8.** (−7, −4)
9. (−5, 6) **10.** (8, 2)
11. *y*-axis **12.** *x*-axis

13.

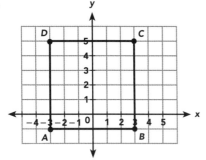

square

14.

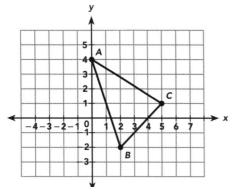

triangle

15.

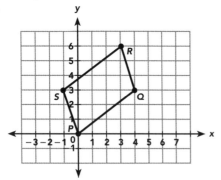

parallelogram

16.

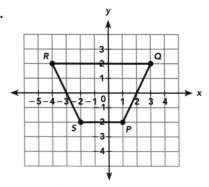

trapezoid

17. a)

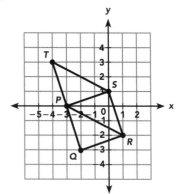

b) *Q* (−2, −3)
c) *T* (−4, 3)

18. a)

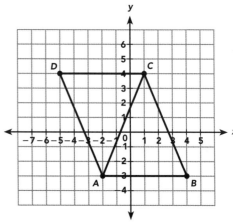

b) isosceles triangle
c) *D* (−5, 4)

Lesson 9.2
1. *AB* = 5 units
2. *CD* = 7 units
3. *EF* = 6 units
4. *GH* = 6 units
5. *JK* = 5 units

6. $MN = 3$ units

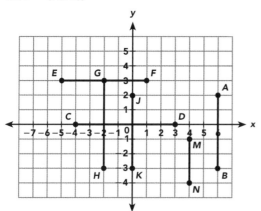

7. a) $B(7, -1)$, $C(7, 2)$
   b) $B(-5, -1)$, $C(-5, 2)$

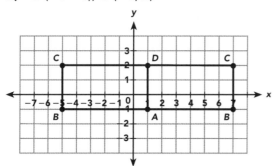

8. a) $G(-2, 5)$, $H(2, 5)$
   b) $G(-2, -3)$, $H(2, -3)$

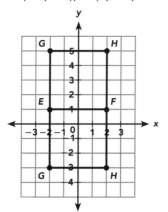

9. a) right scalene triangle
   b) $D(-2, 5)$

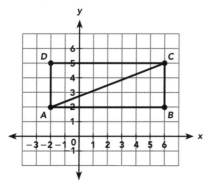

10. $P(-20, 10)$, $Q(5, 10)$, $R(5, -15)$,
     $S(25, -15)$, $T(25, -25)$,
     $U(-20, -25)$
11. 155 feet
12. $V(10, -15)$, $W(15, -15)$
13. 1,075 square feet
14. $A(-20, 20)$, $B(20, 20)$, $C(-20, -8)$
15. $D(0, 20)$, $E(8, 20)$, $F(8, 12)$, $G(0, 12)$

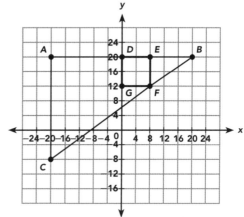

16. $40 + 49 + 28 = 117$
   The perimeter of the playground is
   approximately 117 yards.
17. $117 - 12 = 105$
   $105 \div 5 = 21$
   It will take her 21 seconds to get to point B.

Lesson 9.3
1. 24; 48; 60

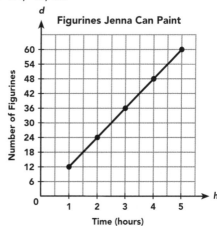

   a) linear/straight line graph
   b) 30 figurines
   c) 4.5 hours
   d) $h \geq 4$
   e) d is dependent variable, and
       h is independent variable.

2. a) 40; 30; 10

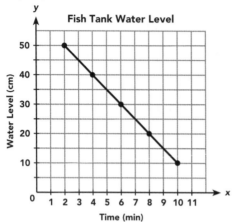

b) 45 centimeters
c) 7 minutes
d) 12 minutes
e) 5 centimeters per minute

3. a) 80; 110; 140

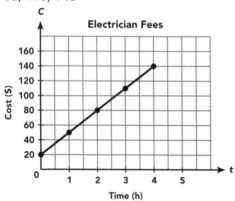

b) $65
c) 2.5 hours
d) $95 ÷ 2.5 = 38$
   $38 per hour
e) $C \geq 20$

Brain @ Work

1. a)

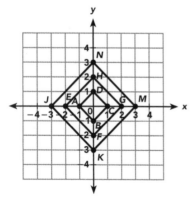

   i. square
   ii. square
   iii. square

b) Area of $ABCD = \left(\dfrac{1}{2} \cdot 2 \cdot 1\right) \cdot 2$

   $= 2$ square centimeters

   Area of $EFGH = \left(\dfrac{1}{2} \cdot 4 \cdot 2\right) \cdot 2$

   $= 8$ square centimeters

   Area of $JKMN = \left(\dfrac{1}{2} \cdot 6 \cdot 3\right) \cdot 2$

   $= 18$ square centimeters

c) The area of figure $ABCD$ is 2 times the square of 1.
   The area of figure $EFGH$ is 2 times the square of 2.
   The area of figure $JKMN$ is 2 times the square of 3.
   $1^2 \times 2 = 2$
   $2^2 \times 2 = 8$
   $3^2 \times 2 = 18$

Chapter 10

Lesson 10.1

1. Answers vary. Sample:
   base: AB; height: AC
2. Answers vary. Sample:
   base: PR; height: QT
3. Answers vary. Sample:

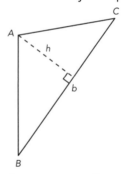

4. Answers vary. Sample:

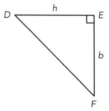

5. Answers vary. Sample:

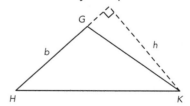

6. Answers vary. Sample:

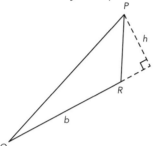

7. $\frac{1}{2} \cdot 14 \cdot 8 = 56$ square inches

8. $\frac{1}{2} \cdot 7 \cdot 18 = 63$ square centimeters

9. $\frac{96 \cdot 2}{16} = 12$ centimeters

10. $\frac{96 \cdot 2}{8} = 24$ centimeters

11. $\frac{135 \cdot 2}{15} = 18$ yards

12. $\frac{135 \cdot 2}{27} = 10$ yards

13. $\frac{1}{2} \cdot 26 \cdot 12 = 156$ square feet

14. $28 \cdot 3 = 84$ square inches

15. Base of the shaded region
$= 96 \div 3 = 32$ in.
Area of the shaded region
$= \frac{1}{2} \cdot 32 \cdot 16 = 256$ square inches

16. Area of $XYZ = \frac{1}{2} \cdot 18 \cdot 12$
$= 108$ in.^{2}
Area of $WZY = \frac{1}{2} \cdot 12 \cdot (18 - 13)$
$= 30$ in.^{2}
Area of $WXY = 108 - 30$
$= 78$ square inches
      OR
Area of $WXY = \frac{1}{2} \cdot 13 \cdot 12$
$= 78$ square inches

17. $EN = 9 \cdot 2 - 12 = 6$ in.
Area of triangle EMN
$= \frac{1}{2} \cdot 6 \cdot 9$
$= 27$ square inches

18.

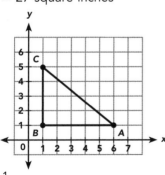

$\frac{1}{2} \cdot 5 \cdot 4 = 10$ square units

19.

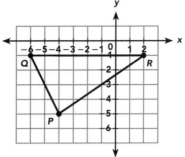

$\frac{1}{2} \cdot 8 \cdot 4 = 16$ square units

20.

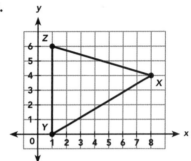

$\frac{1}{2} \cdot 6 \cdot 7 = 21$ square units

21.

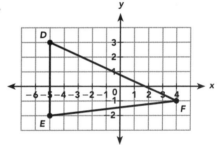

$\frac{1}{2} \cdot 5 \cdot 9 = 22.5$ square units

22.

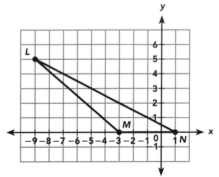

$\frac{1}{2} \cdot 4 \cdot 5 = 10$ square units

23.

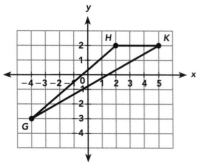

$\frac{1}{2} \cdot 3 \cdot 5 = 7.5$ square units

24. Base of triangle $HKM = \sqrt{64} = 8$ in.
Height of triangle $HKM = \sqrt{144} - 8 = 4$ in.
Area of triangle $HKM = \frac{1}{2} \cdot 8 \cdot 4 = 16$ in.^{2}
Area of the figure
$= 144 + 64 + 16$
$= 224$ square inches

25. Length of 1 side $= 160 \div 4$
$= 40$ in.
By observation, triangles PQM and NPS
together make up $\frac{1}{2}$ of the square, and
triangle MNR make up $\frac{1}{8}$ of the square.
$1 - \frac{1}{2} - \frac{1}{8} = \frac{8}{8} - \frac{4}{8} - \frac{1}{8} = \frac{3}{8}$
So, the area of triangle PMN is $\frac{3}{8}$ the area
of $PQRS$.
Area of triangle PMN
$= \frac{3}{8} \cdot 40 \cdot 40$
$= 600$ square inches

26. Length of the small square
$= 16 - 12 = 4$ in.
Area of the larger square
$= 4\left(\frac{1}{2} \cdot 16 \cdot 12\right) + 4 \cdot 4 = 400$ in.^{2}
Side length of the larger square
$= \sqrt{400} = 20$ inches

Lesson 10.2

1.

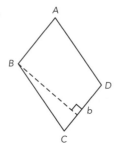

2.

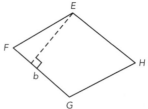

3. Answers vary. Sample:

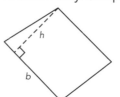

4. Answers vary. Sample:

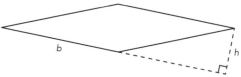

5. $26 \cdot 18 = 468$ square inches
6. $14 \cdot 23 = 322$ square feet
7.

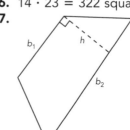

8.

9. $\frac{1}{2} \cdot 12(15 + 20)$
$= 210$ square inches

10. $\frac{1}{2} \cdot 11(14 + 18)$
$= 176$ square centimeters

11. $207 \div 9 = 23$ inches
12. $112 \div 16 = 7$ inches
13. $\frac{1}{2}h(10 + 17) = 108$
$h = 108 \cdot 2 \div 27$
$= 8$ centimeters

14. $\frac{1}{2}h(30 + 20) = 375$
$h = 375 \cdot 2 \div 50$
$= 15$ feet

15.

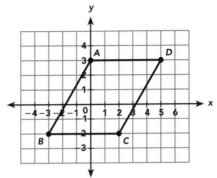

The coordinates of point C are $(2, -2)$.
Base = 5 units, height = 5 units
Area of parallelogram $ABCD$
= $5 \cdot 5 = 25$ square units

16.

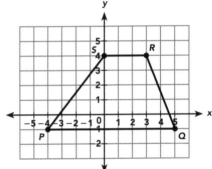

$RS = 3$ units, $PQ = 9$ units,
height = 5 units
Area of trapezoid $PQRS$
= $\frac{1}{2} \cdot 5(3 + 9) = 30$ square units

17. $\frac{1}{2} \cdot 8(JN + 20) = 136$

$4(JN + 20) = 136$
$JN = 136 \div 4 - 20 = 14$ miles

18. $\frac{1}{2} \cdot h(20 + 28) = 312$

$h = 312 \cdot 2 \div 48$
    = 13 yards
Area of triangle ABC
= $\frac{1}{2} \cdot 20 \cdot 13 = 130$ square yards

Lesson 10.3

1. 7 triangles

2. 10 triangles

3. Area of a triangle
= $\frac{1}{2} \cdot 17.5 \cdot 12$
= 105 cm²
Area of the pentagon
= $5 \cdot 105$
= 525 square centimeters

4. Area of a triangle
= $\frac{1}{2} \cdot 12 \cdot 10.3$
= 61.8 in.²
Area of the hexagon
= $6 \cdot 61.8$
= 370.8 square inches

5. The pentagon is made up of 5 identical triangles.
Area of each triangle
= $292.5 \div 5 = 58.5$ ft²
1 side of the pentagon
= $\frac{58.5 \cdot 2}{9} = 13$ feet

6. The hexagon is made up of 6 identical triangles.
Area of each triangle
= $93.6 \div 6 = 15.6$ in.²
Height of each triangle
= $\frac{15.6 \cdot 2}{6} = 5.2$ in.
Height of the hexagon
= $5.2 \cdot 2 = 10.4$ inches

7. Area of the hexagon
= $3 \cdot (7 \cdot 6)$
= 126 square centimeters

8. Area of a triangle
= $\frac{1}{2} \cdot 8.4 \cdot 13$
= 54.6 cm²
Area of the polygon
= $54.6 \cdot 10$
= 546 square centimeters

9. Area of trapezoid $ABGH$
= Area of trapezoid $CDEF$
= $\frac{1}{2}(10 + 24) \cdot 7$
= 119 cm²
Area of rectangle $BCGF$
= $24 \cdot 10$
= 240 cm²
Area of the polygon
= $119 + 119 + 240$
= 478 square centimeters

10. Area of triangle OAB
= $\frac{1}{2} \cdot 18 \cdot 26$
= 234 cm²
Area of the pentagon
= $234 \cdot 5$
= 1,170 cm²
Area of triangle AEF
= $\frac{1}{2} \cdot 42.3 \cdot 24.7$
= 522.405 cm²
Area of the figure
= $1,170 + 522.405$
= 1,692.405 square centimeters

Lesson 10.4

1. bh; sum of the areas of the two triangles

2. $\frac{1}{2}h(b_1 + b_2)$; sum of the areas of the two triangles

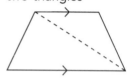

3. Sum of the areas of the 5 identical triangles; sum of the areas of an isosceles triangle, two right triangles, and a rectangle

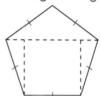

4. Sum of the areas of two trapezoids

5. Sum of the areas of a triangle and a trapezoid

6. a)

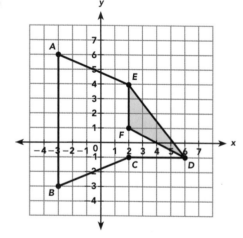

b) The area of figure ABCDE is formed by a trapezoid and a triangle.
Area of trapezoid ABCE
$= \frac{1}{2} \cdot 5(5 + 9)$
$= 35$ square units

Area of the triangle CDE
$= \frac{1}{2} \cdot 4 \cdot 5$
$= 10$ square units
Area of figure ABCDE
$= 35 + 10$
$= 45$ square units

c) There are five units along EC. So, point F is three units from E. The coordinates of point F are (2, 1).

7. Height of the triangle
$= \frac{28 \cdot 2}{8} = 7$ cm
Area of parallelogram PQRS
$= 20 \cdot 7 = 140$ square centimeters

8. Area of square CDEF
$= 7 \cdot 7 = 49$ in.²
Area of trapezoid ABCF
$= \frac{1}{2} (19 - 7)(16 + 7) = 138$ in.²
Area of figure ABCDE
$= 49 + 138 = 187$ square inches

9. Area of parallelogram PQTU
$= 10 \cdot 13 = 130$ in.²
Area of trapezoid QRST
$= \frac{1}{2} \cdot 12(18 + 10) = 168$ in.²
Area of figure
$= 130 + 168 = 298$ square inches

10. Height of parallelogram ABCE
$= \frac{135}{15} = 9$ in.
Area of triangle CDE
$= \frac{1}{2} \cdot 9(20 - 15) = 22.5$ in.²
Area of trapezoid ABDE
$= 135 + 22.5 = 157.5$ square inches

11. $6 \cdot 6 \cdot 3 = 108$ square centimeters

12. $32 \cdot 32 = 1,024$ in.²
Area of the shaded region
$= \frac{3}{8}$ of the area of the square
$= \frac{3}{8} \cdot 32 \cdot 32$
$= 384$ square inches

13. Area of the shaded region
$= \frac{1}{2} \cdot 8 \cdot 8 = 32$ in.²
Area of the unshaded region
$= 32 \cdot 14 = 448$ square inches

14. Area of trapezoid *CDEG*
$= \frac{1}{2} \cdot 20(36 + 20) = 560$ in.²
Area of triangle *BCG*
$= \frac{1}{2} \cdot 36 \cdot 36 = 648$ in.²
Area of triangle *BDE*
$= \frac{1}{2} \cdot 20(36 + 20) = 560$ in.²
Area of the shaded region
$= 560 + 648 - 560$
$= 648$ square inches

15. a) *PS* = 7 units, *PQ* = 4.5 units
Perimeter of *PQRS*
$= 7 \cdot 2 + 4.5 \cdot 2 = 23$ units
23 units → 138 in.
1 unit → 138 ÷ 23 = 6 in.
Length of each small rectangle
= 3.5 units
3.5 · 6 = 21 in.
Area of each small rectangle
= 21 · 6
= 126 square inches
b) 126 · 9 = 1,134 in.²
The area of rectangle *PQRS* is
1,134 square inches.

16.
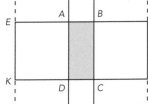
By observation:
Area of *EFGA* = area of *ABCD*
Length of square *FHCK*
= perimeter of *ABCD* ÷ 2
= 30 ÷ 2 = 15 in.
Area of square *FHCK*
= 15 · 15 = 225 in.²
Total area of square *ADKE* and square *ABHG*
= 234 ÷ 2 = 117 in.²
Area of rectangle *ABCD*
= (225 − 117) ÷ 2
= 54 in.²
The area of rectangle *ABCD* is
54 square inches.

Brain @ Work
1. a) Each equilateral triangle can be divided
into 9 smaller equilateral triangles.
Area of each smaller triangle
= 18 ÷ 9 = 2 cm²
Area of the shaded region is formed by
six smaller equilateral triangles
= 6 · 2 = 12 square centimeters

b) Area of composite figure
$= 18 \cdot 2 - 12$
$= 24$ square centimeters

2. a)
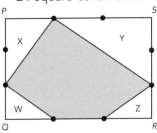
Area of *PQRS*
$= 18 \cdot 12 = 216$ in.²
Area of triangle X
$= \frac{1}{2} \cdot 6 \cdot 8 = 24$ in.²
Area of triangle Y
$= \frac{1}{2} \cdot 12 \cdot 8 = 48$ in.²
Area of triangle W
= area of triangle Z
$= \frac{1}{2} \cdot 6 \cdot 4 = 12$ in.²
Shaded region
$= 216 - (24 + 48 + 12 + 12)$
$= 120$ square inches
b) One equal part
$= 120 \div 2 = 60$ in.²
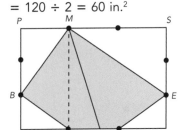
Area of triangle *MBA*
$= \frac{1}{2} \cdot 12 \cdot 6 = 36$ in.²
Area of triangle *AMN*
$= 60 - 36 = 24$ in.²
Length of base $\overline{AN}$
$= \frac{24 \cdot 2}{12} = 4$ in.
Length of $\overline{QN}$
$= 6 + 4 = 10$ inches

> **Chapter 11**

Lesson 11.1
1. 2 · 3.14 · 11 = 69.08 inches
2. 3.14 · 50 = 157 centimeters
3. Length of the semicircular arc
$\approx \frac{1}{2} \cdot \frac{22}{7} \cdot 42 = 66$ cm

Distance around the semicircle
= 66 + 42 = 108 centimeters

4. Length of the semicircular arc

$\approx \frac{1}{2} \cdot 2 \cdot \frac{22}{7} \cdot 0.77 = 2.42$ in.

Distance around the semicircle

$= 2.42 + 0.77 + 0.77 = 3.96$ inches

5. Length of the arc of the quadrant

$\approx \frac{1}{4} \cdot 2 \cdot 3.14 \cdot 10$

$= 15.7$ cm

Distance around the quadrant

$= 15.7 + 10 + 10$

$= 35.7$ centimeters

6. Length of the arc of the quadrant

$\approx \frac{1}{4} \cdot 2 \cdot 3.14 \cdot 21.4$

$= 33.598$ ft

Distance around the quadrant

$= 33.598 + 21.4 + 21.4$

$= 76.398$ feet

7. $2 \cdot \frac{22}{7} \cdot 1.9 = 11\frac{33}{35}$ feet

8. $\frac{22}{7} \cdot 25 = 78\frac{4}{7}$ inches

9. $\frac{22}{7} \cdot 18 = 56\frac{4}{7}$ millimeters

10. $\frac{1}{2} \cdot \frac{22}{7} \cdot 25 = 39\frac{2}{7}$ in.

Distance around the semicircle

$= 39\frac{2}{7} + 25$

$= 64\frac{2}{7}$ inches

11. $\frac{1}{4} \cdot 2 \cdot \frac{22}{7} \cdot 11 = 17\frac{2}{7}$ cm

Distance around the quadrant

$= 17\frac{2}{7} + 11 + 11$

$= 39\frac{2}{7}$ centimeters

12. $\frac{3}{4}$ of the circle

$\approx \frac{3}{4} \cdot 2 \cdot 3.14 \cdot 18$

$= 84.78$ cm

Distance around the figure

$= 84.78 + 18 + 18$

$= 120.78$ centimeters

13. Length of the arcs of the 4 quadrants

$\approx 2 \cdot 3.14 \cdot 15$

$= 94.2$ in.

Distance around the figure

$= 94.2 + 15 + 15$

$= 124.2$ inches

14. Length of semicircular arc

$\approx \frac{1}{2} \cdot 3.14 \cdot 18 = 28.26$ yd

Distance around the shaded region

$= 28.26 + 18 \cdot 3$

$= 82.26$ yards

15. Length of the arc of the quadrant

$\approx \frac{1}{4} \cdot 2 \cdot 3.14 \cdot 20 = 31.4$ cm

Distance around the shaded region

$= 31.4 + 20 + 20$

$= 71.4$ centimeters

16. Length of the 2 semicircular arcs

$\approx \frac{22}{7} \cdot 7 = 22$ in.

Distance around the shaded region

$= 22 + 12 + 12 = 46$ inches

17. Length of the small semicircular arc

$\approx \frac{1}{2} \cdot \frac{22}{7} \cdot 140 = 220$ cm

Length of the big semicircular arc

$\approx \frac{1}{2} \cdot \frac{22}{7} \cdot (140 + 35 + 35) = 330$ cm

Distance around the shaded region

$= 220 + 330 + 35 + 35$

$= 620$ centimeters

18. Length of the arc of the 2 quadrants

$\approx \frac{1}{2} \cdot 2 \cdot \frac{22}{7} \cdot 7 = 22$ cm

Distance around the figure

$= 22 + 7 + 7 + 2 + 2$

$= 40$ centimeters

Lesson 11.2

1. $3.14 \cdot 20 \cdot 20$

$= 1{,}256$ square centimeters

2. $3.14 \cdot 4 \cdot 4$

$= 50.24$ square miles

3. $\frac{1}{2} \cdot \frac{22}{7} \cdot 17.5 \cdot 17.5$

$= 481.25$ square feet

4. $\frac{1}{2} \cdot \frac{22}{7} \cdot 56 \cdot 56$

$= 4{,}928$ square meters

5. $\frac{1}{4} \cdot 3.14 \cdot 3.5 \cdot 3.5$

≈ 9.6 square inches

6. $\frac{1}{4} \cdot 3.14 \cdot 14 \cdot 14$

≈ 153.9 square yards

7. $\frac{1}{2} \cdot \frac{22}{7} \cdot 20 \cdot 20$

$= 628\frac{4}{7}$ square meters

8. $\frac{1}{2} \cdot \frac{22}{7} \cdot 7 \cdot 7 = 77$ square centimeters

9. a) Area of 6-inch pizza

$\approx \dfrac{22}{7} \cdot 3 \cdot 3 \approx 28.29$ in.^{2}

Area of 12-inch pizza

$\approx \dfrac{22}{7} \cdot 6 \cdot 6 \approx 113.14$ in.^{2}

$113.14 - 28.29 = 84.85$

The area of the 6-inch pizza is 84.85 square inches less than the area of the 12-inch pizza.

b) Cost of 6-inch pizza per square inch

$= \$3.50 \div 28.29 \approx \$0.12$

Cost of 12-inch pizza per square inch

$= \$11 \div 113.14 \approx \$0.10$

The 12-inch pizza is a better deal because it costs less per square inch than the 6-inch pizza.

10. Area of the semicircular flowerbed

$\approx \dfrac{1}{2} \cdot \dfrac{22}{7} \cdot 42 \cdot 42 = 2,772$ in.^{2}

Area of the circular fishpond

$\approx \dfrac{22}{7} \cdot 21 \cdot 21 = 1,386$ in.^{2}

Area of flowerbed without the pond

$\approx 2,772 - 1,386$

$= 1,386$ square inches

11. Area of the shaded region

$= 21 \cdot 21 = 441$ square inches

OR

Area of the quadrant

$\approx \dfrac{1}{4} \cdot \dfrac{22}{7} \cdot 21 \cdot 21 = 346.5$ in.^{2}

Area of shaded region in the square

$\approx 21 \cdot 21 - \dfrac{1}{4} \cdot \dfrac{22}{7} \cdot 21 \cdot 21$

$= 94.5$ in.^{2}

Total area of the shaded regions

$= 346.5 + 94.5 = 441$ square inches

12. Radius $= 45 \div 3 = 15$ cm

Area of the figure

$\approx 3.14 \cdot 15 \cdot 15$

$= 706.5$ square centimeters

13. Area of the quadrant

$\approx \dfrac{1}{4} \cdot 3.14 \cdot 18 \cdot 18$

$= 254.34$ in.^{2}

Area of the semicircle

$\approx \dfrac{1}{2} \cdot 3.14 \cdot 9 \cdot 9$

$= 127.17$ in.^{2}

Area of the shaded region

$= 254.34 - 127.17$

$= 127.17$ square inches

14. Radius of the circle

$= 48 \div 2 = 24$ cm

Area of the circle

$\approx 3.14 \cdot 24 \cdot 24$

$= 1,808.64$ cm^2

Radius of each semicircle

$= 48 \div 4 \div 2 = 6$ cm

Total area of the 4 semicircles

$=$ area of 2 circles

$\approx 2 \cdot (3.14 \cdot 6 \cdot 6)$

$= 226.08$ cm^2

Area of the shaded region

$= 1,808.64 - 226.08$ cm^2

$= 1,582.56$ square centimeters

15. Area of the bigger circle

$\approx 3.14 \cdot 10 \cdot 10 = 314$ cm^2

Area of the smaller circle

$\approx 3.14 \cdot 7 \cdot 7 = 153.86$ cm^2

Area of the shaded region

$= \dfrac{2}{7} \cdot 153.86 = 43.96$ cm^2

Area of the unshaded region

$= 314 + 153.86 - 2 \cdot 43.96$ cm^2

$= 379.94$ square centimeters

Lesson 11.3

1. Area

$\approx 3.14 \cdot 36 \cdot 36$

$= 4,069.44$ square inches

Circumference

$\approx 3.14 \cdot 72 = 226.08$ inches

2. Area

$\approx 3.14 \cdot 1.2 \cdot 1.2$

$= 4.52$ square meters

Circumference

$\approx 3.14 \cdot 2.4 = 7.54$ meters

3. One round of the can

$\approx 2 \cdot \dfrac{22}{7} \cdot 9.8 = 61.6$ cm

100 rounds of the can

$= 61.6 \cdot 100$

$= 6,160$ cm $= 61.6$ m

The length of the piece of wire is 61.6 meters.

4. One revolution

$\approx \dfrac{22}{7} \cdot 0.7 = 2.2$ meters

$440 \div 2.2 = 200$

The wheel makes 200 revolutions if the bicycle travels 440 meters.

5. Area of the inner circle
$\approx 3.14 \cdot 7 \cdot 7$
$= 153.86$ ft²
Area of the outer circle
$\approx 3.14 \cdot (7 + 2) \cdot (7 + 2)$
$= 254.34$ ft²
Area of the walkway
$= 254.34 - 153.86$
$= 100.48$ square feet
OR
Area of the walkway
$\approx 3.14 \cdot (9 \cdot 9 - 7 \cdot 7)$
$= 100.48$ square feet

6. a) Distance around the shaded part
of the rug = circumference of a circle
$\approx 2 \cdot 3.14 \cdot 50$
$= 314$ cm
The distance around the shaded part of
the rug is 314 centimeters.
b) Area of the shaded part of the rug
$=$ area of 2 squares
$= 50 \cdot 50 \cdot 2$
$= 5,000$ cm²
The area of the shaded part of the rug is
5,000 square centimeters.

7. Radius of the shaded circle
$= 56 \div 4 = 14$ cm
Area of the shaded circle
$\approx 3.14 \cdot 14 \cdot 14 = 615.44$ cm²
Area of shaded part above $\overline{AB}$
$\approx 56 \cdot 28 - \dfrac{1}{2} \cdot 3.14 \cdot 28 \cdot 28$
$= 337.12$ cm²
Total area of the shaded region
$= 615.44$ cm² $+ 337.12$ cm²
$= 952.56$ cm²
The area of the shaded region is
952.56 square centimeters.

8. a) Rounded to the nearest whole number:
$100 \div 14 \approx 7$
$60 \div 14 \approx 4$
$7 \cdot 4 = 28$
Alex can cut 28 badges.
b) Area of 28 badges
$\approx 28 \left(\dfrac{22}{7} \cdot 7 \cdot 7 \right)$
$= 4,312$ cm²
Area of the rectangular cardboard
$= 100 \cdot 60 = 6,000$ cm²
Area of the cardboard left over
$= 6,000 - 4,312$
$= 1,688$ square centimeters

9. a) Diameter of the outer semicircle
$= 40 + (2 \cdot 3.5)$
$= 47$ m

Circumference of the two inner
semicircles
$\approx \dfrac{22}{7} \cdot 40$ m $= 125\dfrac{5}{7}$ m
Circumference of the two outer
semicircles
$\approx \dfrac{22}{7} \cdot 47$ m $= 147\dfrac{5}{7}$ m
Adam runs farther than Joe.
b) Difference in 1 round
$= 147\dfrac{5}{7} - 125\dfrac{5}{7} = 22$ m
Difference in 2 rounds
$= 22 \cdot 2 = 44$ m
Adam runs 44 meters farther than Joe.

Brain @ Work

1. Radius $= AC = BD = 10$ cm
Height of triangle ABD
$= \dfrac{1}{2} \cdot 10 = 5$ cm
Area of the quadrant
$\approx \dfrac{1}{4} \cdot 3.14 \cdot 10 \cdot 10 = 78.5$ cm²
$2 \cdot$ area of triangle ABD
$= 2 \cdot \dfrac{1}{2} \cdot 10 \cdot 5 = 50$ cm²
Area of the shaded region
$= 78.5$ cm² $- 50$ cm²
$= 28.5$ square centimeters

2. Area of square $PQRS$
$= 8 \cdot 8 = 64$ in.²
Area of square $ABCD$
$= 2 \cdot$ area of square $PQRS$
$= 2 \cdot 64$
$= 128$ square inches

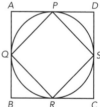

3.

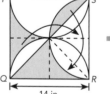 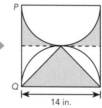

Area of the triangle
$= \dfrac{1}{2} \cdot 14 \cdot 7 = 49$ in.²
Area of the rectangle
$= 14 \cdot 7 = 98$ in.²
Area of the semicircle
$\approx \dfrac{1}{2} \cdot \dfrac{22}{7} \cdot 7 \cdot 7 = 77$ in.²
Area of rectangle $-$ area of semicircle
$= 98 - 77 = 21$ in.²
Area of the shaded region
$= 49 + 21 = 70$ in.²
The total area of the shaded parts is
70 square inches.

4. a) Area of fishpond
   = area of square *ABCD* − area of the circle
   $\approx 7 \cdot 7 - \dfrac{22}{7} \cdot \dfrac{7}{2} \cdot \dfrac{7}{2}$
   $= 10\dfrac{1}{2}$ square feet

b) Area of the 4 flowerbeds = area of the circle − area of the 4 triangles
   $\approx \dfrac{22}{7} \cdot \dfrac{7}{2} \cdot \dfrac{7}{2} - 4\left(\dfrac{1}{2} \cdot \dfrac{7}{2} \cdot \dfrac{7}{2}\right)$
   = 14 square feet

Cumulative Practice
for Chapters 8 to 11

1.

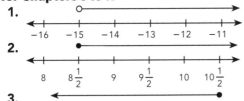

2.

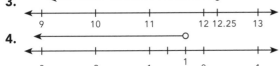

3.

4.

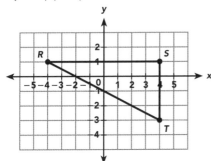

5. a) *S* (4, 1)
   b) *T* (4, −3)

6. $\dfrac{1}{2} \cdot 24 \cdot 9 = 108$ square inches

7. $\dfrac{1}{2} \cdot 8 \cdot 28 = 112$ square centimeters

8. $\dfrac{60 \cdot 2}{8} = 15$ inches

9. $\dfrac{60 \cdot 2}{12} = 10$ inches

10. $19 \cdot 13 = 247$ square inches

11. $\dfrac{1}{2} \cdot 14(13 + 17) = 210$ square feet

12. Area of a triangle
   $= \dfrac{1}{2} \cdot 18 \cdot 12 = 108$ cm²
   Area of the pentagon
   $= 5 \cdot 108 = 540$ square centimeters

13. Area of a triangle
   $= \dfrac{1}{2} \cdot 16 \cdot 15 = 120$ in.²
   Area of the hexagon
   $= 6 \cdot 120 = 720$ square inches

14. $2 \cdot \dfrac{22}{7} \cdot 21 = 132$ inches

15. $3.14 \cdot 30 = 94.2$ centimeters

16. Length of semicircular arc
   $\approx \dfrac{1}{2} \cdot \dfrac{22}{7} \cdot 49 = 77$ in.
   Perimeter
   $= 77 + 49 = 126$ inches

17. Length of the arc of the quadrant
   $\approx \dfrac{1}{4} \cdot 2 \cdot 3.14 \cdot 20 = 31.4$ in.
   Perimeter
   $= 31.4 + 20 + 20 = 71.4$ inches

18. $\dfrac{1}{4} \cdot 3.14 \cdot 8 \cdot 8$
   $= 50.24$ square inches

19. Radius = 20 ÷ 2 = 10 cm
   $\dfrac{1}{2} \cdot 3.14 \cdot 10 \cdot 10$
   $= 157$ square inches

20. $\dfrac{22}{7} \cdot 21 \cdot 21$
   $= 1{,}386$ square centimeters

21. $\dfrac{3}{4} \cdot \dfrac{22}{7} \cdot 14 \cdot 14$
   $= 462$ square centimeters

22. Area of the base
   $\approx 3.14 \cdot 6 \cdot 6$
   $= 113.04$ square centimeters

23. $\dfrac{1}{2} \cdot \dfrac{22}{7} \cdot r^2 = 77$
   $r^2 = \dfrac{77 \cdot 7}{11} = 49$
   $r = \sqrt{49} = 7$ ft
   Diameter of the semicircle
   $= 2 \cdot 7 = 14$ feet

24. $132 = 2 \cdot \dfrac{22}{7} \cdot r$
   $132 = \dfrac{44}{7} \cdot r$
   $r = \dfrac{132 \cdot 7}{44} = 21$ in.
   The radius of the circular hoop is 21 inches.

25. $\dfrac{x}{4} = 12$
   $x = 12 \cdot 4 = 48$
   Faye has 48 yards of ribbon.

26. a) Son's age now = y − 25
   $n = (y + 12) + (y - 25 + 12)$
   $n = 2y - 1$
   b) $n = 2 \cdot 38 - 1 = 75$

27. Mick has $\frac{5}{11}k$ fewer shirts than LaToya.

28. Perimeter of the square
$$= 9p \cdot 4 = 36p \text{ in.}$$
Perimeter of the rectangle
$$= 36p \div 3 = 12p \text{ in.}$$
Width of the rectangle
$$= 12p \div 6 = 2p \text{ in.}$$
The width of the rectangle is $2p$ inches.

29. 12 hours $\rightarrow 2 \cdot 3.14 \cdot 8$
$$= 50.24 \text{ cm}$$
24 hours $\rightarrow 50.24 \cdot 2$
$$= 100.48 \text{ cm}$$
The tip of the hour hand travels 100.48 centimeters in one day.

30. $\frac{1}{2} \cdot h(12 + 18) = 255$
$$30h = 255 \cdot 2$$
$$h = 510 \div 30$$
$$= 17 \text{ in.}$$
The height of trapezoid $WXYZ$ is 17 inches.

31. Length of the shaded regions
$$= 40 - 6 = 34 \text{ yd}$$
Width of the shaded regions
$$= 30 - 6 = 24 \text{ yd}$$
Area of the shaded regions
$$= 34 \cdot 24 = 816 \text{ yd}^2$$
The area of the shaded regions is 816 square yards.

32. Area of triangle BCE
$$= \frac{1}{2} \cdot 18 \cdot 6 = 54 \text{ cm}^2$$
Area of rectangle $ABCD$
$$= 54 - 12 = 42 \text{ cm}^2$$
$$AB = 42 \div 6 = 7 \text{ centimeters}$$

33. The total area of the shaded regions is equal to the sum of the area of a circle and the area of a rectangle.
Area of a circle
$$\approx \frac{22}{7} \cdot 14 \cdot 14 = 616 \text{ in.}^2$$
Area of rectangle $OPQR$
$$= 28 \cdot 14 = 392 \text{ in.}^2$$
Total area of the shaded regions
$$= 616 + 392 = 1{,}008 \text{ in.}^2$$
The total area of the shaded regions is 1,008 square inches.

34. Area of triangle ABC
$$= \frac{1}{2} \cdot 15 \cdot 36 = 270 \text{ in.}^2$$
Area of triangle ACD
$$= \frac{1}{3} \text{ of area of triangle } ABC$$
$$= \frac{1}{3} \cdot 270 = 90 \text{ square inches}$$

35.

a) Base = 6 units;
height = 8 units
Area of triangle PQR
$$= \frac{1}{2} \cdot 6 \cdot 8 = 24 \text{ square units}$$

b) The coordinates of point S are (8, 5).

c) Area of parallelogram $PQRS$
$$= 6 \cdot 8 = 48 \text{ square units}$$

d) Area of triangle TQR
$$= 24 \div 2 = 12 \text{ square units}$$
So, $TQ = (12 \cdot 2) \div 6$
$$= 4 \text{ units}$$
Point T has the same x-coordinate as point Q and is 4 units above point Q. So, the coordinates of point T are $(-3, 1)$.

36. a)

Number of cards (n)	0	5	10	15	20	25
Total cost (C dollars)	10	20	30	40	50	60

b)

c) $70
d) $410
e) $n \le 20$
f) Dependent variable: C; independent variable: n

37. a) $45m \le 480; \; m \le 10\frac{2}{3}$

b) $m \le 10\frac{2}{3}$

No, 11 is not a possible value of m.

c)

The maximum value of m is 10.

38. The area of rectangle $BCDE$ is 4 times the area of triangle ABF.

So, area of triangle ABF
$= 90 \div 5 = 18$ ft²

$\frac{1}{2} \cdot AB \cdot BF = 18$ ft²

$AB \cdot BF = 18 \cdot 2 = 36$ ft²

$AB = BF = \sqrt{36} = 6$ ft

$AC = 2 \cdot 6 = 12$ feet

39. Area of triangle RQT
$= \frac{1}{2} \cdot 21 \cdot 10 = 105$ in.²

Area of square $PQRS$
$= 21 \cdot 21 = 441$ in.²

Area of circle
$\approx \frac{22}{7} \cdot \frac{21}{2} \cdot \frac{21}{2} = 346.5$ in.²

Total area of the shaded regions
$= 105 + 441 - 346.5$
$= 199.5$ square inches

40.

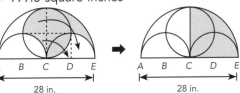

Half of the region is shaded.
The area of the shaded regions is formed by a quadrant.

$\frac{1}{4} \cdot \frac{22}{7} \cdot 14 \cdot 14$
$= 154$ square inches

Chapter 12

Lesson 12.1

1. cube

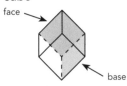

2. triangular prism

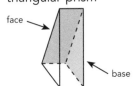

3. square pyramid

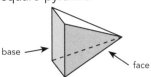

4. triangular pyramid

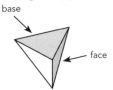

5. rectangular prism   **6.** triangular prism
7. square pyramid   **8.** square pyramid
9. No   **10.** No
11. Yes   **12.** No
13. Yes   **14.** Yes
15. Answers vary. Sample:

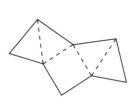

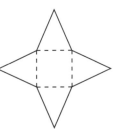

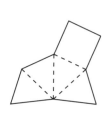

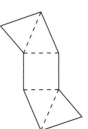

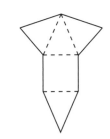

16.

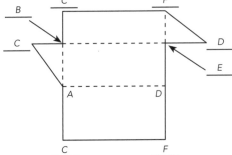

Lesson 12.2

1. Area of one square face
   = 9 · 9 = 81 in.^{2}
   Surface area of cube
   = 81 · 6 = 486 in.^{2}
   The surface area of the cube
   is 486 square inches.

2. Area of two rectangular bases
   = 2 · (20 · 8) = 320 ft^2
   Total area of the other four rectangular faces
   = (20 + 8 + 20 + 8) · 6
   = 336 ft^2
   Surface area of rectangular prism
   = 320 + 336 = 656 ft^2
   The surface area of the rectangular shipping
   container is 656 square feet.

3. Area of two triangular bases
   $= 2 \cdot \left(\frac{1}{2} \cdot 4 \cdot 7 \right) = 28$ cm^2
   Total area of three rectangular faces
   = (4 + 7.3 + 7.3) · 12 = 223.2 cm^2
   Surface area of prism
   = 28 + 223.2 = 251.2 cm^2
   The surface area of the prism is
   251.2 square centimeters.

4. Area of two triangular bases
   $= 2 \cdot \left(\frac{1}{2} \cdot 16 \cdot 12 \right) = 192$ in.^{2}
   Area of the other three rectangular faces
   = (20 + 12 + 16) · 4
   = 192 in.^{2}
   Surface area of container
   = 192 + 192 = 384 in.^{2}
   The surface area of the cheese is
   384 square inches.

5. Area of two trapezoidal bases
   $= 2 \cdot \left[\frac{1}{2} \cdot 20 \cdot (10 + 17) \right] = 540$ cm^2
   Area of four rectangular faces
   = (20 + 10 + 21.2 + 17) · 24
   = 1,636.8 cm^2
   Surface area of prism
   = 540 + 1,636.8 = 2,176.8 cm^2
   The surface area of the block of wood is
   2,176.8 square centimeters.

6. Area of large triangular base
   $= \frac{1}{2} \cdot 8 \cdot 6.9 = 27.6$ in.^{2}
   Area of small triangular base
   $= \frac{1}{2} \cdot 5 \cdot 4.3 = 10.75$ in.^{2}
   Area of three trapezoidal faces
   $= 3 \cdot \left[\frac{1}{2} \cdot 15 \cdot (8 + 5) \right] = 292.5$ in.^{2}

Surface area of solid
= 27.6 + 10.75 + 292.5
= 330.85 in.^{2}
The surface area of the solid is
330.85 square inches.

7. Area of one pentagonal base
   $= (120 \cdot 8) + \frac{1}{2} \cdot 120 \cdot (19 - 8)$
   = 1,620 ft^2
   Area of two pentagonal bases
   = 2 · 1,620 = 3,240 ft^2
   Area of two rectangular faces
   = 2 · (125 · 8) = 2,000 ft^2
   Total area of walls to be painted
   = (3,240 + 2,000) − 225 = 5,015 ft^2
   The total area of the walls that need to be
   painted is 5,015 square feet.

8. a) Each base of the prism has $\frac{m}{2}$ sides.

   b) The prism has $1\frac{1}{2}m$ edges.

   c) The prism has $\left(2 + \frac{m}{2} \right)$ faces.

Lesson 12.3

1. Volume = 8^3 = 512 in.^{3}
   The volume of the cube is 512 cubic inches.

2. Volume = 3.5 · 1.8 · 2 = 12.6 ft^3
   The volume of the box is 12.6 cubic feet.

3. Area of triangular base
   $= \frac{1}{2} \cdot 9 \cdot 12 = 54$ in.^{2}
   Volume = 54 · 20 = 1,080 in.^{3}
   The volume of the gift box is
   1,080 cubic inches.

4. Volume of each cube
   = 3^3 = 27 in.^{3}
   There are 13 cubes.
   Volume of solid = 27 · 13 = 351 in.^{3}
   The volume of the solid is 351 cubic inches.

5. No. Ovals will have different dimensions with
   other cuts.

6. No. Rectangles will have different dimensions
   with other cuts.

7. Yes.

8. Edge length of cube = $\sqrt[3]{512}$ = 8 cm
   Area of each face = 8^2 = 64 cm^2
   The area of each face of the cube is
   64 square centimeters.

9. Area of square base = 5,880 ÷ 30 = 196 in.^{2}
   Side length of square base = $\sqrt{196}$ = 14 in.
   The side length of the square base is
   14 inches.

10. Volume of rectangular prism
$= 12 \cdot 6 \cdot 3 = 216$ in.³
Edge length of cube $= \sqrt[3]{216} = 6$ in.
The edge length of the cube is 6 inches.

11. Area of trapezoidal base
$= \dfrac{1}{2} \cdot 5 \cdot (3 + 10) = 32.5$ in.²
Volume of prism $= 32.5 \cdot 28 = 910$ in.³
The volume of the prism is 910 cubic inches.

12. Height of prism $= 10 \div 5 \cdot 9 = 18$ ft
Volume of prism $= 78.5 \cdot 18 = 1{,}413$ ft³
The volume of the prism is 1,413 cubic feet.

13. Volume of smaller prism
$= 4 \cdot 4 \cdot 30 = 480$ cm³
Volume of solid
$= (12 \cdot 12 \cdot 30) - 480$
$= 3{,}840$ cm³
The volume of the solid is
3,840 cubic centimeters.

Lesson 12.4

1. Area of two triangular bases
$= 2 \cdot \left(\dfrac{1}{2} \cdot 6 \cdot 4 \right) = 24$ ft²
Surface area = (area of two triangular bases)
$+ (5 + 5 + 6) \cdot h$
$136 = 24 + 16 \cdot h$
$136 - 24 = 24 + 16h - 24$
$112 = 16h$
$7 = h$
The height of the prism is 7 feet.

2. Height of empty portion of tank
$= 30 - 18 = 12$ cm
Volume of water needed
$= 60 \cdot 40 \cdot 12 = 28{,}800$ cm³
The volume of water needed is
28,800 cubic centimeters.

3. Volume of wall $= 450 \cdot 18 \cdot 108$
$= 874{,}800$ cm³
Number of bricks
$= 874{,}800 \div 972 = 900$
There are 900 bricks in the wall.

4. Volume of Box A
$= 18 \cdot 12 \cdot 10 = 2{,}160$ in.³
Volume of Box B
$= 2{,}160 \div 2 = 1{,}080$ in.³
Volume of Box B $= 72 \cdot h$
$1{,}080 = 72h$
$15 = h$
The height of Box B is 15 inches.

5. a) Area of base
$= (20 \cdot 15) - (8 \cdot 7) = 244$ in.²
Volume $= 244 \cdot 10 = 2{,}440$ in.³
The volume of the prism is
2,440 cubic inches.

b) Area of two bases $= 2 \cdot 244 = 488$ in.²
Surface area
$= 488 + (20 + 15 + 20 + 7 + 7$
$+ 15) \cdot 10$
$= 1{,}328$ in.²
The surface area of the prism is
1,328 square inches.

6. a) Volume of water in tank
$= 30 \cdot 25 \cdot 6 = 4{,}500$ cm³
Volume of water in pail
$= 4{,}500 \div 9 \cdot 4 = 2{,}000$ cm³
Capacity of pail
$= 2{,}000 \div 4 \cdot 5 = 2{,}500$ cm³
The capacity of the pail is
2,500 cubic centimeters.

b) Volume of water needed to fill tank
$= 30 \cdot 25 \cdot (36 - 6)$
$= 22{,}500$ cm³
Minimum number of pails of water needed
$= 22{,}500 \div 2{,}500 = 9$
The minimum number of pails needed to
fill the tank completely is 9.

7. a) Surface area $= \dfrac{1}{2} \cdot 50 \cdot (1.5 + 8) \cdot 2 +$
$(1.5 + 50 + 8 + 50.4) \cdot x$
$3{,}222.5 = 475 + 109.9x$
$3{,}222.5 - 475 = 109.9x + 475 - 475$
$2747.5 = 109.9x$
$25 = x$
The measure of x is 25 meters.

b) Area of each trapezoidal base
$= \dfrac{1}{2} \cdot 50 \cdot (1.5 + 8) = 237.5$ m³
Volume of pool
$= 237.5 \cdot 25 = 5{,}937.5$ m³
The volume of the pool is
5,937.5 cubic meters.

8. a) $\dfrac{2}{3} - \dfrac{1}{4} = \dfrac{5}{12}$
3,000 cubic inches of water fills $\dfrac{5}{12}$
of the tank.
Capacity of the tank $= 3{,}000 \div 5 \cdot 12$
$= 7{,}200$ in.³
The capacity of the tank is
7,200 cubic inches.

b) Area of square base $= 20^2 = 400$ in.²
Height of tank $= 7{,}200 \div 400 = 18$ in.
Height of the water $= \dfrac{2}{3} \cdot 18 = 12$ in.
The height of the water is 12 inches.

Brain @ Work

1. a) The side length of each identical square is the height of the box.

Height (in.)	Length (in.)	Width (in.)	Volume (in.³)
1	28	18	504
2	26	16	832
3	24	14	1,008
4	22	12	1,056
5	20	10	1,000
6	18	8	864

The maximum volume of the box is 1,056 cubic inches.

b) From part **a)**, the side length of each identical square is 4 inches.

2. a) Number of cubes
$$= 1 + 4 + 9 + 16 + 25 = 55$$
Volume of cube $= 3^3 = 27$ in.³
Volume of solid $= 27 \cdot 55 = 1,485$ in.³
The volume of the solid is 1,485 cubic inches.

b) Number of faces from the top view or bottom view = 25
Number of faces from the front view or back view = 15
Number of faces from the left view or right view = 15
Total number of faces
$$= (25 + 15 + 15) \cdot 2 = 110$$
Surface area of solid
$$= (3^2) \cdot 110 = 990 \text{ in.}^2$$
The surface area of the solid is 990 square inches.

Chapter 13

Lesson 13.1

1.

Model	Frequency
A	12
B	11
C	9
D	8

a) Number of customers
$$= 12 + 11 + 9 + 8 = 40$$
There were 40 customers who took part in the survey.

b) Number of customers $= 12 - 8 = 4$
4 more customers prefer model *A* than model *D*.

c) $\dfrac{12}{40} \times 100\% = 30\%$
30% of the customers surveyed stated model *A* as their favorite.

2.

Sport	Frequency
Basketball	10
Soccer	6
Hockey	5
Swimming	15

a) Number of students
$$= 10 + 6 + 5 + 15 = 36$$
36 students were questioned.

b) Number of students $= 15 + 5 = 20$
20 students named swimming or hockey as their favorite Olympic sport.

c) Percent $= \dfrac{6}{36} \times 100\% = 16\dfrac{2}{3}\%$
$16\dfrac{2}{3}\%$ of the students named soccer as their favorite Olympic sport.

3. a) 0, 1, 2, 2, 2, 2, 2, 3, 3, 3, 3, 3, 3, 3, 3, 3, 4, 4, 4, 5, 5, 5, 5, 6, 6, 6, 6

b)

Number of Hours	Tally	Frequency
0–2	ЖІ //	7
3–4	ЖІ ЖІ //	12
5–6	ЖІ ///	8

c) Number of students $= 12 + 8$
$= 20$ students
20 students surf the Internet for more than 2 hours each day.

d) Number of students $= 7 + 12$
$= 19$ students
19 students surf the Internet for less than 5 hours each day.

4. a) 0, 0, 0, 0, 0, 0, 1, 1, 1, 1, 1, 1, 1, 1, 2, 2, 2, 2, 2, 2, 2, 2, 3, 3, 3, 3, 3, 4, 4

b)

Number of Pets	Tally	Frequency
0–1	ЖІ ЖІ ////	14
2–3	ЖІ ЖІ ////	14
4–5	//	2

c) Number of families $= 14 + 2 = 16$
16 families own at least 2 pets.

d) Percent $= \dfrac{2}{30} \times 100\% = 6\dfrac{2}{3}\%$
$6\dfrac{2}{3}\%$ of the families own 4 to 5 pets.

Lesson 13.2

1.

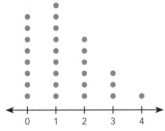

Number of Hours

2. Number of observations
$= 1 + 2 + 5 + 6 + 4 + 2 = 20$
There are 20 observations.

3. Most students spend 2 to 3 hours reading for pleasure.

4. Percent $= \dfrac{2}{20} \times 100\% = 10\%$
10% of the students spend 5 hours reading for pleasure.

5.

Number of Charms

6. Number of observations
$= 8 + 9 + 6 + 3 + 1 = 27$
There are 27 observations.

7. Most students own 0 or 1 mobile phone charm.

8. Percent $= \dfrac{3 + 1}{27} \times 100\% \approx 15\%$
Approximately 15% of the students own more than 2 mobile phone charms.

9. Number of students
$= 2 + 4 + 6 + 4 + 2 + 2 = 20$
The number of students surveyed is 20.

10. Most students watched 2 movies.

11. Percent $= \dfrac{4 + 2 + 2}{20} \times 100\% = 40\%$
40% of the students watched at least three movies.

12. The dot plot has a "tail" on the right. Most of the data are from 1 to 3, and the distribution is slightly right skewed. The data spans from 0 to 5.
Range: $5 - 0 = 5$
From the description of the dot plot, most of the students saw about 1 to 3 movies, and all of them saw 0 to 5 movies.

13. Number of students
$= 1 + 2 + 4 + 8 + 5 + 2 + 2 + 1 = 25$
25 students took the quiz.

14. Percent $= \dfrac{2 + 2 + 1}{25} \times 100\% = 20\%$
20% of the students scored at least 8 points.

15. Most students scored 6 points.

16. The dot plot is nearly symmetrical. These data show a nearly symmetrical dot plot centered around 6. Most of the data falls between 5 and 7. The data spans from 3 to 10.
Range: $10 - 3 = 7$
From the description of the dot plot, most of the students scored between 5 and 7 points.

17. Number of observations
$= 4 + 8 + 4 + 2 + 1 + 1 = 20$
There are 20 observations.

18. Percent $= \dfrac{4 + 8}{20} \times 100\% = 60\%$
60% of the students have less than 2 board games.

19. Let x be the number of new children who were surveyed.

$$\frac{5}{7}(20 + x) = 12 + x$$

$$\frac{5}{7}(20) + \frac{5}{7}x = 12 + x$$

$$14\frac{2}{7} + \frac{5}{7}x = 12 + x$$

$$-\frac{2}{7}x = -2\frac{2}{7}$$

$$x = 8$$

8 more children were surveyed.

Lesson 13.3

1.

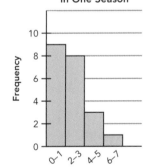

Number of Goals Scored in One Season

2.

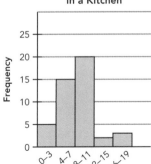

Number of Spoons in a Kitchen

3.

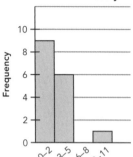

Number of Computers in a Laboratory

4.

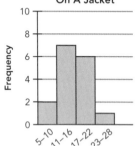

Number Of Buttons On A Jacket

5. $2 + 6 + 10 + 8 + p = 30$
$26 + p = 30$
$p = 4$

The value of p is 4.

6.

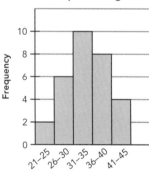

Time Taken by Students to Complete Assignment

The data shows that most students completed the mathematics assignment in between 31 minutes to 35 minutes. The range of the data is 24. The data are well spread and the shape of the histogram is nearly symmetrical.

7. Percent $= \dfrac{8 + 4}{30} \times 100\% = 40\%$

40% of the students took at least 36 minutes to complete their assignment.

8. Number of observations
$= 16 + 12 + 8 + 4 = 40$
There are 40 observations.

9. Percent $= \dfrac{16 + 12}{40} \times 100\% = 70\%$

70% of the students live at most 6 miles from the school.

10. There are 40 students in the group. Most students live 1 to 3 miles from the school. The range of the data is 11. The histogram has a "tail" to the right. Most of the data is to the right of the interval 1–3, the shape of the histogram is right-skewed.

11. 4 students have a bill greater than $30.

12. Fraction $= \dfrac{11 + 3 + 1}{30} = \dfrac{1}{2}$

$\dfrac{1}{2}$ of the students paid at least $21 for their phone bills.

13. Most students have a phone bill between $11 and $30. The range of the data is $59. The histogram has a tail to the left. Most of the data is to the left of the interval 21–30, the shape of the histogram is left-skewed. There is 1 student who has a phone bill between $51 and $60, which is an outlier in the data.

14.

Duration (min)	0–29	30–59	60–89	90–119
Frequency	2	4	7	7

15.

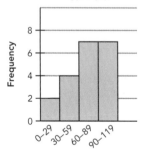

Parking Durations in a Car Park

16. Percent $= \dfrac{7 + 7}{20} \times 100\% = 70\%$

70% of the parking durations are greater than 59 minutes.

17. Most of the parking durations are between 60 minutes and 119 minutes. The range of the data is 119. The histogram has a "tail" to the left. Most of the data is to the left of the interval 90–119, the shape of the histogram is left-skewed.

18. $12 + y + 10 = 36$
$y + 22 = 36$
$y = 36 - 22 = 14$

$1 + 2 + x + 6 + 12 + y + 10 = 50$
$x + y + 31 = 50$
$x + 14 + 31 = 50$
$x + 45 = 50$
$x = 50 - 45$
$= 5$

The value of x is 5, and the value of y is 14.

19.

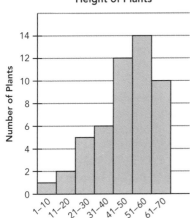

Height of Plants

20. Percent $= \dfrac{1 + 2 + 5}{50} \times 100\% = 16\%$

16% of the plants are in poor health.

21.

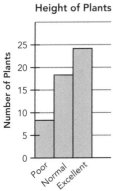

Height of Plants

22. The first histogram, which uses more intervals, reveals more about the distribution of data. It shows the three intervals that contain the most data. This histogram will be more useful when you want to find out the height intervals of the tallest plants.

The second histogram, which uses fewer intervals with greater width, categorizes the plants into poor, normal, and excellent growth. This histogram will be more useful when you want general information on whether the plants are growing well.

Brain @ Work

1. When there are equal intervals, each bar width should be equal. However, the intervals are unequal. The width of the interval 6–9 is 2 times the other intervals. So, the frequency for this bar has to be divided by 2.

2.

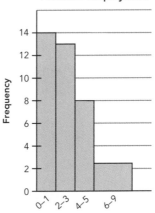

Teachers' Employment

Chapter 14

Lesson 14.1

1. Mean $= \dfrac{9 + 10 + 11 + 16 + 12 + 12 + 14}{7}$
$= 12$

2. Mean
$= \dfrac{20 + 22 + 21 + 23 + 25 + 24 + 26 + 28 + 27}{9}$
$= 24$

3. Mean $= \dfrac{17.4 + 20.3 + 84.1 + 31.2 + 53.7 + 11.7}{6}$
$= 36.4$

4. Mean $= \dfrac{3.8 + 5.2 + 4.8 + 5.0 + 4.6}{5} = 4.68$

The mean height of these five peacocks is 4.68 feet.

5. Mean
$= \dfrac{\begin{array}{l}11.3 + 15.2 + 12.0 + 13.6 + \\ 12.8 + 10.9 + 14.2 + 14.0\end{array}}{8}$
$= 13$

The mean time these paper airplanes stayed in the air is 13 seconds.

6. Mean $= \dfrac{9 + 5 + 7 + 9 + 5}{5} = 7$

The mean number of pins that fell is 7.

7. Number of girls
$= 1 + 2 + 1 + 5 + 3 + 4 + 2 = 18$
There are 18 girls in the group.

8. Total number of headbands
$= 1 \cdot 4 + 2 \cdot 5 + 1 \cdot 6 + 5 \cdot 7 + 3 \cdot 8 + 4 \cdot 9 + 2 \cdot 10$
$= 135$
The total number of headbands is 135.

9. Mean $= 135 \div 18 = 7.5$
   The mean number of headbands each girl owns is 7.5.

10. Sum of 8 numbers $= 83 \cdot 8 = 664$
    Sum of 4 numbers $= 14 \cdot 4 = 56$
    Mean $= \dfrac{664 + 56}{8 + 4} = 60$
    The mean of the combined set of numbers is 60.

11. Total number of pillows $= 13 \cdot 9 = 117$
    Number of pillows in the last box
    $= 117 - (12 + 10 + 15 + 12 + 13 + 15$
    $+ 11 + 13)$
    $= 117 - 101 = 16$
    There are 16 pillows in the last box.

12. Total height of 8 plants $= 18 \cdot 8 = 144$ in.
    Total height of 7 plants
    $= 12 + 13 + 15 + 15 + 17 + 23 + 24$
    $= 119$ in.
    Height of last plant $= 144 - 119 = 25$ in.
    The height of the eighth plant is 25 inches.

13. Sum of 6 numbers $= 41 \cdot 6 = 246$
    Sum of 5 numbers $= 46 \cdot 5 = 230$
    Unknown number $= 246 - 230 = 16$
    The unknown number is 16.

14. Sum of 7 numbers $= 21 \cdot 7 = 147$
    Sum of 5 numbers
    $= 18 + 23 + 21 + 17 + 19$
    $= 98$
    Sum of unknown 2 numbers $= 147 - 98$
    $= 49$
    Let x be one of the unknown numbers.
    So the other unknown number is $\frac{3}{4}x$.
    $x + \dfrac{3}{4}x = 49$
    $1\dfrac{3}{4}x = 49$
    $x = 28$
    $\dfrac{3}{4}x = 21$
    The two unknown numbers are 21 and 28.

15. Sum of 9 numbers $= 6 \cdot 9 = 54$
    Sum of 7 numbers $= 6 \cdot 7 = 42$
    Sum of unknown 2 numbers
    $= 54 - 42 = 12$
    Let x be the greater unknown number.
    So the other unknown number is $(x - 4)$.
    $x + x - 4 = 12$
    $2x = 12 + 4$
    $x = 8$
    The greater unknown number is 8.

16. Sum of set of 12 numbers
    $= 5.5 \cdot 12 = 66$
    Sum of set of 8 numbers $= 8k$
    Sum of combined set $= 8.5 \cdot 20$
    $66 + 8k = 170$
    $k = 13$
    The value of k is 13.

Lesson 14.2

1. First, arrange the numbers from least to greatest:
   3, 5, 6, 7, 9, 9, 11
   The median of the data set is the middle value, which is 7.

2. First, arrange the numbers from least to greatest:
   18, 19, 20, 22, 25, 25, 27, 28, 30
   The median of the data set is the middle value, which is 25.

3. First, arrange the numbers from least to greatest:
   2.4, 2.6, 3.5, 4.8, 5.6, 6.5, 8.4, 9.5
   Then find the mean of the two middle values
   $= \dfrac{4.8 + 5.6}{2} = 5.2$
   The median of the data set is 5.2.

4. First, arrange the numbers from least to greatest:
   $3\dfrac{1}{2}, 3\dfrac{3}{4}, 4\dfrac{1}{4}, 4\dfrac{3}{4}, 5\dfrac{7}{12}, 6\dfrac{1}{4}$
   Next, identify the two middle values:
   $4\dfrac{1}{4}$ and $4\dfrac{3}{4}$
   Then find the mean of the two middle values
   $= \left(4\dfrac{1}{4} + 4\dfrac{3}{4}\right) \div 2 = 4\dfrac{1}{2}$
   The median of the data set is $4\dfrac{1}{2}$.

5. First, arrange the sweatshirt sizes from least to greatest:
   8, 8, 10, 10, 10, 12, 14, 14, 16
   The median size of sweatshirts for sale is the middle value, which is 10.

6. First, arrange the number of fish from least to greatest:
   3, 3, 4, 5, 5, 5, 6, 6, 7, 8
   Next, identify the two middle values: 5 and 5
   The median number of fish caught is 5.

7. Total number of students
   $= 6 + 3 + 5 + 5 + 2 = 21$
   There are 21 students.

8. Mean $= \dfrac{6 + 3 \cdot 2 + 5 \cdot 3 + 5 \cdot 4 + 2 \cdot 5}{21} \approx 2.7$

9. The median number of countries visited is 3.

10. Median. The distribution is almost uniform. Also, the mean, 2.7 countries, is unrealistic in this context.

11. Arrange the numbers from the least to the greatest:

13, 34, 43, q, 52, 64

Median $= \dfrac{q + 43}{2}$

$47 = \dfrac{q + 43}{2}$

$q = 51$

The value of q is 51.

12. Arrange the numbers from the least to the greatest:

20, 22, 23, 24, 25, b, 28, 29, 30, 30, 32, 32

Median $= \dfrac{b + 28}{2}$

$27 = \dfrac{b + 28}{2}$

$b = 26$

The value of b is 26.

13. Arrange the numbers from least to greatest:

2, 4, 4, 5, x, 8, 9, 9, 10, y

Median $= \dfrac{x + 8}{2}$

$7 = \dfrac{x + 8}{2}$

$x = 6$

Mean $= \dfrac{2 + 4 + 4 + 5 + 6 + 8 + 9 + 9 + 10 + y}{10}$

$7 = \dfrac{57 + y}{10}$

$y = 13$

The value of x is 6, and the value of y is 13.

14. a) $x + \dfrac{1}{8}$

b) $x - 9\dfrac{1}{4}$

c) $-5.8x + 3$

d) $2x - 1$

e) x

f) x

Lesson 14.3

1. In the data set, the number 4 appears most frequently. So, the number 4 is the mode of the data set.

2. In the data set, the number 12 appears most frequently. So, the number 12 is the mode of the data set.

3. The modes of the data set are 7.7 and 9.3.

4. The mode of the data set is 0.

5. The mode of the data set is oranges.

6.

Number of Apples

7. Total number of apples

$= 6 \cdot 101 + 8 \cdot 102 + 3 \cdot 103$
$\quad + 3 \cdot 104 + 105$

$= 2{,}148$

Mean $= \dfrac{2{,}148}{21} \approx 102$

8. The median number of apples is 102.

9. The modal number of apples is 102.

10. a) The possible values of x are 7, 8, 9, and 12.

b) A possible value of x is 10. The mode is 10.

OR

A possible value of x is 11. The mode is 11.

11. a) $1 + 4 + 6 + x + 8 + y + 2 = 30$

$x + y = 9$

The greatest value of x is 7, so the value of y is 2.

b) The median number of light bulbs that need to be replaced is 3.

c) Mean

$= \dfrac{1 \cdot 4 + 2 \cdot 6 + 3 \cdot 7 + 4 \cdot 8 + 5 \cdot 2 + 6 \cdot 2}{30}$

$= \dfrac{91}{30} \approx 3$

Lesson 14.4

1. First, arrange the numbers from least to greatest:

3, 3, 4, 4, 5, 5, 6, 6, 6, 6, 6, 7, 7, 7, 7

Mean

$= \dfrac{2 \cdot 3 + 2 \cdot 4 + 2 \cdot 5 + 5 \cdot 6 + 4 \cdot 7}{15}$

$= \dfrac{82}{15} \approx 5.5$

The mean mass of honey harvested is approximately 5.5 gallons.

The median mass of honey harvested is 6 gallons.

The modal mass of honey harvested is 6 gallons.

2. Mean
$$= \frac{3 \cdot 3 + 4 \cdot 6 + 5 \cdot 14 + 6 \cdot 15 + 7 \cdot 7 + 8 \cdot 5}{50}$$
$$= \frac{282}{50} = 5.64$$

The mean number of windows is
5.64 windows.
The median number of windows is 6.
The modal number of windows is 6.

3. Median and mode. The mean number of
windows is 5.64. It is not a realistic number
for describing the data set. The median and
mode are both 6, which is a realistic number
for describing the data set. So, the median
and the mode best describe the data set.

4. Mean
$$= \frac{1 \cdot 3 + 2 \cdot 7 + 3 \cdot 5 + 2 \cdot 2}{3 + 3 + 7 + 5 + 2}$$
$$= \frac{36}{20} = 1.8$$

The mean number of hours is 1.8 hours.
The median number of hours is 2. The modal
number of hours is 2.

5. Mean
$$= \frac{1 \cdot 3 + 2 \cdot 7 + 3 \cdot 5 + 2 \cdot 2 + 7}{3 + 3 + 7 + 5 + 2 + 1}$$
$$= \frac{43}{21} \approx 2.05 > 2$$

The least number is 7.

6. The shape of the distribution is right-skewed.
So, the measure of center is likely to be
17 degrees Celsius, which is in the
middle range.

7. Mean
$$= \frac{\begin{array}{c} 7 + 13 + 2 \cdot 14 + 3 \cdot 15 + \\ 5 \cdot 16 + 3 \cdot 17 + 2 \cdot 18 \end{array}}{1 + 1 + 2 + 3 + 5 + 3 + 2}$$
$$= \frac{260}{17} \approx 15$$

The mean number of public holidays is
approximately 15 days.
The median number of public holidays is 16.
The modal number of public holidays is 16.

8. There is an outlier, 7.

9. Median and mode. The mean number of
public holidays is 15, which is affected by
the outlier at 7. The median and mode is 16,
which is the same. So, the median and the
mode best describe the data set.

10. The data are well spread and the shape of
the data distribution is nearly symmetrical
with an outlier, 7. So, the measure of
center is likely to be 16, which is in the
upper range.

11.

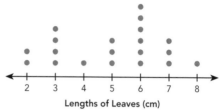

Lengths of Leaves (cm)

12. There are two peaks in the distribution of
the data—one is for length 3 centimeters,
and the other is for length 6 centimeters.
Most of the data is to the left of the length
6 centimeters, and the distribution is
left-skewed. So, the measure of center is
likely to be 5 centimeters, which is in the
middle range.

Brain @ Work

1. Let the missing numbers be x and y.
Total number of members
$= 102 + 104 + 75 + 70 + x + y$
$92\frac{1}{6} \cdot 6 = x + y + 351$
$553 = x + y + 351$
$553 - 351 = x + y$
$x + y = 202$
Total number of members
$= 102 + 104 + 75 + 70 + 0.75x + y$
$87\frac{5}{6} \cdot 6 = 0.75x + y + 351$
$527 = 0.75x + y + 351$
$527 - 351 = 0.75x + y$
$0.75x + y = 176$
25% of $x = 202 - 176 = 26$
$x = 26 \cdot 4 = 104$
$y = 202 - 104 = 98$
The two missing numbers are 98 and 104.

Cumulative Practice
for Chapters 12 to 14

1. c   **2.** b   **3.** a

4. Surface area
$= (2 \cdot 12^2) + (4 \cdot 12 \cdot 3)$
$= 288 + 144$
$= 432 \text{ in.}^2$
Volume $= 12^2 \cdot 3$
$= 432 \text{ in.}^3$

5. Surface area
$= (2 \cdot \frac{1}{2} \cdot 14 \cdot 7) + 10 \cdot (9.2 + 10.6 + 14)$
$= 98 + 338$
$= 436 \text{ cm}^2$
Volume $= \frac{1}{2} \cdot 14 \cdot 7 \cdot 10$
$= 490 \text{ cm}^3$

6. edge $= \sqrt{\frac{232}{15}} \approx 3.9 \text{ m}$

7. edge $= \sqrt{\dfrac{232}{2}} \approx 10.8$ m

8. The solid is made up of 12 cubes.
Volume of the solid $= 12(4 \cdot 4 \cdot 4) = 768$ in.^{3}
The volume of the solid is 768 cubic inches.

9. The solid is made up of 9 cubes.
Volume of each cube $= 243 \div 9 = 27$ in.^{3}
Edge length $= \sqrt[3]{27} = 3$ in.

Total number of faces
$= 5 + 5 + 6 + 6 + 4 + 4 = 30$
Surface area $= 3^2 \cdot 30 = 270$ in.^{2}
The surface area of the solid
is 270 square inches.

10. Arrange the ages from least to greatest:
8, 10, 10, 12, 14, 15, 15, 16
Mean
$= \dfrac{8 + 10 + 10 + 12 + 14 + 15 + 15 + 16}{8}$

$= \dfrac{100}{8}$

$= 12.5$
The mean age is 12.5 years.

Median $= \dfrac{12 + 14}{2} = \dfrac{26}{2} = 13$

The median age is the mean of the two
middle values, which is 13 years.

11. Arrange the times from the least to
the greatest:
55.4, 55.5, 55.6, 55.7, 55.9, 55.9, 56.0, 56.2,
56.3, 56.5
Mean
$= (55.4 + 55.5 + 55.6 + 55.7 + 2 \cdot 55.9$
$\quad + 56.0 + 56.2 + 56.3 + 56.5) \div 10$

$= \dfrac{559}{10}$

$= 55.9$ s
The median time is the middle value,
which is 55.9 seconds.

12. Arrange the durations of the songs from the
least to the greatest:
$1\dfrac{4}{15}, 2, 2\dfrac{8}{15}, 3\dfrac{1}{3}, 3\dfrac{8}{15}, 4, 4\dfrac{1}{3}, 5\dfrac{11}{30}, 5\dfrac{2}{3}, 5\dfrac{2}{3}, 5\dfrac{4}{5}, 6$
Mean
$= \left(1\dfrac{4}{15} + 2 + 2\dfrac{8}{15} + 3\dfrac{1}{3} + 3\dfrac{8}{15} + 4\right.$

$\left. + 4\dfrac{1}{3} + 5\dfrac{11}{30} + 5\dfrac{2}{3} + 5\dfrac{2}{3} + 5\dfrac{4}{5} + 6\right) \div 12$

$= 49\dfrac{1}{2} \div 12 = 4\dfrac{1}{8}$ min

The mean duration is $4\dfrac{1}{8}$ minutes.

Median $= \left(4 + 4\dfrac{1}{3}\right) \div 2 = 4\dfrac{1}{6}$ min

The median duration is the mean of the two
middle values, which is $4\dfrac{1}{6}$ minutes.

13.

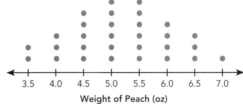
Weight of Peach (oz)

14.

Weight of Peach (oz)	3.5–4.0	4.5–5.0	5.5–6.0	6.5–7.0
Frequency	5	11	10	4

15.

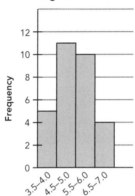
Weights of 30 Peaches

Most peaches weigh between 4.5 ounces to
6 ounces. The range of the data is 3.5.
The histogram is nearly symmetrical. Most of
the data falls between 4.5 and 6.0. The data
spans from 3.5 to 7.0.

16. There are 29 people in the group.
Most of the people waited 4 to 9 minutes for
a taxi. The histogram has a "tail" on
the left, and the shape of the histogram
is left-skewed.

17.

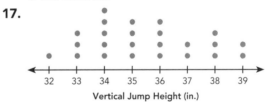
Vertical Jump Height (in.)

18. Mean
$= (32 + 3 \cdot 33 + 5 \cdot 34 + 4 \cdot 35$
$\quad + 4 \cdot 36 + 2 \cdot 37 + 3 \cdot 38 + 2 \cdot 39) \div 24$

$= \dfrac{851}{24} \approx 35$ in.

The median vertical jump height is the
middle value, which is 35 inches.
The modal vertical jump height is 34 inches.

19.

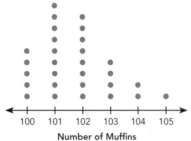

Number of Muffins

20. Mean
$$= (5 \cdot 100 + 10 \cdot 101 + 8 \cdot 102$$
$$+ 4 \cdot 103 + 2 \cdot 104 + 105) \div 30$$
$$= 101.7 \approx 102$$
The mean number of muffins is about 102.

Median $= \dfrac{101 + 102}{2} = 101.5 \approx 102$

The median number of muffins is about 102.
The modal number of muffins made is 101.

21. Area of triangle
$$= \frac{1}{2} \cdot x \cdot 18$$
$$= 9x \text{ square inches}$$
Area of square base $= \dfrac{9x}{3} \cdot 4$
$$= 12x \text{ square inches}$$
Surface area $= 12x + 4 \cdot 9x$
$$576 = 12x + 36x$$
$$= 48x$$
$$x = 576 \div 48 = 12$$
The length of the edge of the square base is 12 inches.

22. a) Volume $= 160 \cdot 80 \cdot \left(\dfrac{5}{8} - \dfrac{1}{4} \right) \cdot x$
$$156{,}000 = 4{,}800x$$
$$x = 156{,}000 \div 4{,}800 = 32.5$$
The height of the container is 32.5 centimeters.

b) Surface area
$$= 160 \cdot 80 + 2 \cdot 160 \cdot 32.5$$
$$+ 2 \cdot 80 \cdot 32.5$$
$$= 28{,}400 \text{ cm}^2$$
The amount of glass used to make the bottom and sides of the container is 28,400 square centimeters.

23. a) Total number of offices
$$= 3 + a + 8 + 5 + 1$$
$$= 17 + a$$
$$25 = 17 + a$$
$$a = 8$$
The value of a is 8.

b)

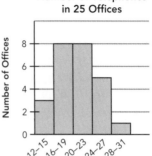

Number of Telephones

There are 25 offices. Most of the offices have 16 to 23 telephones. Most of the data is near the center of the range, and the histogram is nearly symmetrical.

c) Percent $= \dfrac{5 + 1}{25} \times 100\%$
$$= 24\%$$

d) Percent $= \dfrac{3 + 8}{25} \times 100\%$
$$= 44\%$$

24. a) Number of students
$$= 14 + p + 8$$
$$= 22 + p$$
$$37 = 22 + p$$
$$p = 15$$

Total numbers of students
$$= 2 + q + 8 + 37$$
$$= 47 + q$$
$$52 = 47 + q$$
$$q = 5$$

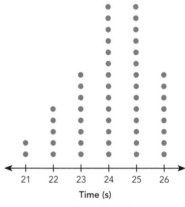

Time (s)

b) Mean $= \dfrac{\begin{array}{c} 2 \cdot 21 + 5 \cdot 22 + 8 \cdot 23 + \\ 14 \cdot 24 + 15 \cdot 25 + 8 \cdot 26 \end{array}}{52}$
$$= \dfrac{1{,}255}{52} \approx 24 \text{ s}$$

c) Total time of second set $= 25 \cdot 30 = 750$ s
Mean $= \dfrac{1{,}255 + 750}{82} \approx 24.5$ s